Once a Blue Always a Blue

Once a Blue Always a Blue

The Autobiography of Richard Edghill

Dante Friend

pitch

First published by Pitch Publishing, 2014

Pitch Publishing
A2 Yeoman Gate
Yeoman Way
Durrington
BN13 3QZ
www.pitchpublishing.co.uk

A CIP catalogue record is available for this book from the British Library.

ISBN 978 1-90962-627-0

Typesetting and origination by Pitch Publishing
Printed in Great Britain

CONTENTS

FOREWORD

ACTIONS speak louder than words and Richard Edghill's record speaks volumes. I first saw Richard play at 16 and it was obvious to all he would be a top player. He was technically good, very athletic and very competitive.

He went on to have a great career at a great club. Richard showed tremendous character as captain of City during challenging times for the club he adored and showed loyalty to the club through very difficult times.

He helped the resurrection from League 1 back up to the Premier League. Taking a penalty in the play-off final especially showed great bravery. I felt that was really a defining moment in his career as he was someone not particularly recognised for being a goalscorer but he took on that responsibility when there was so much riding on it and he would have been under extreme pressure.

Let's not forget the pressure got to some of our fans that day, many of them had already left the ground, but bravery is when you are under extreme pressure and you are still prepared to step forward. We knew the pressure on our players and I knew how nervous they were. The team's strength of character, epitomised by Richard, is what got us through.

I know Richard struggled with injuries and he didn't become the England player I had expected, but maybe he will enlighten us in his book. Working with him was a joy as he worked hard and wanted to learn. I am sure with these qualities he will be successful in whatever area he decides in the future. He played an important part in a fabulous history of a real people's club.

Willie Donachie, former Manchester City full-back and Scotland international, and assistant manager to Joe Royle when Richard Edghill was City's club captain.

1

DRAGGING ME DOWN

MY name is Richard Arlon Edghill and I was born in Oldham on 23 September 1974. That particular year saw Oldham affected by boundary changes. The Local Government Act saw the birth of Greater Manchester, and Oldham – a proud major cotton mill town during the industrial revolution which made Lancashire so famous – was no longer officially part of the red rose county.

Around the time of my birth Manchester City had just beaten Liverpool 2-0 in front of 45,000 at Maine Road with goals from Rodney Marsh and Dennis Tueart. This was then followed by a real thumping at Middlesbrough's old Ayresome Park ground, 3-0, before by a 0-0 draw at Brunton Park against Carlisle United who were in the top flight at the time. A totally mixed bag of results in the week of my birth.

Yet isn't that City all over? The time period around my birth illustrates that. City were the only Manchester club in the top flight at the time having despatched the neighbours into the second tier while I was growing in my mother's womb! It was also the season Franny Lee came back to the club and scored the winner for Derby County at Maine Road with an amazing shot from the edge of the box, a famous goal which gave Barry Davies one of his best commentary moments, 'Look at his face…just look at his face!' City's loss was Derby's gain. They won the league that year.

Manchester City traditionally have always been a rollercoaster club and I feel I was born to take part on that ride. My own career was a rollercoaster in itself. Plenty of highs, plenty of lows but things were never dull at the country's most topsy-turvy club.

I was born into a large family with four boys; Matthew, Mark, Lewis and myself.

In terms of my own family, my mother and father have been huge influences on my life. My mother is called Benedetta and she was born in Genoa in northern Italy. She has a crazy, zany side and settled over here in Coppice in Oldham after the war. My father Colin was from St Lucia in the Caribbean. He was a big influence on me and my brothers.

Mum's home area is the home of Genoa FC and Sampdoria – two good teams. I've never been there but I've heard its very nice. My dad has been even though he's got absolutely nothing to do with the place! Almost all of the family – on my mum's side – were over here already so I have not really had a reason to go over I suppose, only curiosity.

There was some kind of split in the family. My mum's mum was already here, my mother and her sister Angela too, and then there was my uncle Guilio who had links to the Granelli ice cream family.

Matthew is my oldest brother. He became a father at the age of just 16 and moved in with his partner Melanie. Mark is the second-oldest and moved out a year later.

Matthew, Mark...you'd think the next two would be called Luke and John given our strict Catholic upbringing but no, Lewis and myself made up the foursome.

Our grandmother was very religious and made us go to church every Saturday when we were very young. We would always call in and see her as we were walking home, usually to try and pick up a bit of pocket money, but then she would drag us down to church and said we had to go, no excuses! She was a very strong-willed woman too, very strict and believed in discipline.

That song 'Our House' by Madness. I can relate to that. 'There's always something happening and it's usually quite loud.' Growing up in our house wasn't bad, it was just stressful at times because we were forever getting under each other's feet and treading on each other's toes.

Secondary school for me was St Augustine's in Oldham. I wasn't particularly academic. To tell the truth I absolutely hated school. The highlight of the day, every day in fact, was being able to have a kickaround at lunchtime. The only other subject I vaguely enjoyed was craft, design and technology...a chance to use my imagination, making things with Mr Glennie!

I still have some friends who go back to my primary school years, from St Patrick's School in Oldham. One of them, Kevin, came to my wedding. I lost touch with most of the guys from primary school and indeed secondary school really because I was always playing and training by the time I got to a certain age and they were all starting to go out on the razzle in town. They went their way, I went mine.

When I was just five or six years old I discovered a mole on my right arm. I found it to be cancerous and had some deep skin grafts to remove it. You do daft things when you are young. There was a scar there, as big as an egg. It would be dressed in plaster from my shoulder down to my right hand but one day when I got home from school it was itching like hell so stupidly I picked up a metal coat hanger and started to scratch it to ease the itchiness.

This burst all the stitches and made a complete horlicks of everything on the inside of the plaster. Everything was matted together and I then had to go and have all the stitches removed which along with the major injury I suffered at Elland Road in 1995 was just about the most painful thing I can ever recall in my life. Touch wood, the cancer has never come back but I am always paranoid about moles.

Typically, my mum and dad would come in from a day's work and a typical scenario might be Matthew standing over Mark holding one of the rings from the oven about to drop it on his head.

Mark was expelled from school for fighting. He wasn't mischievous, he was just very tough. These days he probably wouldn't be expelled. Much worse goes on now. I know, I do some coaching in schools and have seen how some of them behave. Other kids used to have a pop at my brothers all the time because they were different, they looked different and also because they were big strong lads so instantly they became targets.

Matthew was 6ft 4in for example and that in itself offered a challenge to certain people. My brothers would look out for each other so that would end up bringing some conflict as more and more people were occasionally dragged into confrontational situations.

Mark loved doing ju-jitsu and other types of martial arts. He was a fitness fanatic back in the day and even did ballet classes to help keep his legs supple. Mark was a dancer on *The Hit Man and Her*, the famous programme that was on ITV late at night at the weekends which gave an insight into what was going on out in clubland. He would only be 18 or 19 at most and there he was touring the country and dancing on stage with the likes of Peter Waterman and Michaela Strachan...well perhaps not Waterman!

Lewis lost an eye in a crossbow accident when he was very young but unfortunately and understandably that tragedy has had a really negative impact on his life. He was out playing football with friends one day and on the way home came across a crossbow. Boys being boys they were daring each other to do things and fire things at each other and unfortunately for Lewis he lost the sight of one eye at a very early age.

In my opinion this terrible accident affected his self-esteem during his formative years. It's hard enough being a teenager at the best of times but when something like that has happened at such an early age you are perhaps bound to turn round and say, 'Why me?'

By the time he reached 18 he was entitled to compensation which was designed to help him get through the next stage of his life. Unfortunately, be it peer pressure or a feeling inside that he had to prove that he could be a fun guy to be around, the fact he had a few quid brought him into contact with a new set of mates and they helped him blow a lot of his money.

He had anger. I understand that and I love him just as I love all my brothers, but he has had brushes with the law from time to time and you can't help but wonder how things might have been had it not been for that accident. Having lost an eye he was always an easy target for people looking to get a reaction out of him. It's easy to pick on someone like that and to entice them into 'dares' which as well as taking unnecessary risks generally can only breed more anger, resentment, and bitterness I suppose.

Put it this way, Lewis was a very good footballer. Even with one eye he was a good Sunday league player. Football certainly kept me out of trouble and enabled me to keep my feet on the ground. There's a fine line in life and sometimes once fate has dealt its hand then that's that.

Those of you familiar with Oldham's stadium Boundary Park might know the Blue Bell pub in the vicinity of the ground. When I was about 14 or 15 I went down there one night as there was a massive fight between Chadderton and Royton gangs. Mark was involved and picked on. Some of the Oldham hooligans of the time were involved and some of them had far-right tendencies. I wasn't involved as such, more a spectator, but I could see plenty of jumping around and I quickly learnt that Mark could look after himself. I was called a 'black bastard' by someone or another.

Mark had been in the same school as me and was expelled for fighting. However I was never bullied or picked on at school. Maybe people knew I was part of a big family and had lots of brothers. Maybe it was my size – smaller than my brothers which meant I wasn't on the radar for people.

Outside of school in my early years I experienced a little bit of racism. You'd get the odd remark on the street and where I was brought up there were various areas, predominantly white areas, Asian areas and so on. You were told don't go across certain roads. You don't know people in those areas and they tend to stick together. Most people in Oldham are absolutely great and get on with everybody. There was and still is I suppose a bit of an edge around the place at times, like in the town centre at night where there are rival gangs from various areas that tend to end up in the same place at the same time.

My father Colin is an absolute giant of a man. He is black and he had learned to stand up for himself in life. He always used to say to me, 'If someone is picking on you, you need to deal with it yourself,' and he would leave all the brothers to work out our own individual problems. Yes he could have intervened but didn't want us being seen as weak in any way so the message was drummed into me as a kid, 'It's not me they are picking on, it's you. Stand up for yourself and go and sort it out.'

I was quite shy really up until the age of about 17. The progress I was making at City seemed to give me more confidence in life. I liked girls but I wasn't that bothered about them. I didn't go chasing them. They kind of approached me! I was besotted with football, there was nothing else really in my head. I was football crazy!

There was a well known rollerskating rink up near us and we'd go in there at weekends or after school. There was the Roxy cinema in Hollinwood. Having older brothers and walking in at the same time with them meant I would able to sneak in to watch some of the older films. We'd go round the arcades like the other kids. I'd have girls coming up to me, 'My friend likes you, do you want to go out with my friend?' However I was quite laid back about it all. I wasn't even bothered.

You see, girls, gambling, drinking, breaking the rules…it was all boring compared to football!

Even at primary school we would play football every single lunchtime. I was always kicking a ball about. People commented you wouldn't see me without looking down and seeing a ball seemingly attached to my foot. Lunchtime was the only time really at school I could get properly enthusiastic about because I knew I would just be playing football.

I was the best behaved out of all of the brothers and really football saved me from getting into more trouble than I did. I wasn't bothered about doing homework but I was able to avoid getting in with the wrong crowd because I had so much on the go sports-wise. I played a bit of rugby briefly and quite enjoyed that but it wasn't really on the agenda because of my size. Other lads were far more physically developed than me. I was also very good at athletics and I was a very quick sprinter. I would have a go at anything sporty. I loved it. It's a kind of escape from reality, from the boredom at school and maybe that's how it was for other kids who end up making the grade in professional sport.

I wasn't particularly tall but I was athletic, really athletic, and I could jump far higher than people who were much taller than me. I was great at running and this has stayed with me right throughout my life. Later on I used to beat Ian Brightwell in training – that's Ian Brightwell the son of Olympic athletes Anne Packer and Robbie Brightwell I might add…and of course from then on I got the nickname Said Aouita!

Sundays meant playing for my team Slumberland Rangers in the Oldham Sunday League. Playing in midfield at the time I suppose I was spotted more easily but I had lots of tricks, I could go past people and express myself, I was good on the ball and off the ball.

Funnily enough I didn't get the chance to watch a lot of football at home. My dad used to have the front room to himself so of course what was on the television was down to him. Often I'd pop my head round the door and my uncle would be in there with my dad, smoking and drinking cans of Red Stripe!

'What do you want to stay in for?' he'd say. 'It's the summer holidays, go out and play,' and that would be that. Out of the house at 10am and back in around 6pm. With three of us in the same bedroom we got under each other's feet at times so my poor mother was often shouting at us all. There were constant riots especially with the two older ones and arguments over not sharing toys around.

At Christmas we never got everything we wanted but we kind of accepted it. I would ask for *Star Wars* toys and I would get them. I asked for a bike but I never got one. Only Matthew got a bike. We had to all borrow our brother's bike if we wanted to ride.

My mum had a good job with a firm in Manchester which handled stocks and shares. My dad did a lot of lorry driving work. With four children in the house I suppose there's only ever so much money to share around.

Football became a bit of a constant in my life even at that early age. It was the outlet I needed to express myself at that particular time and threw myself into it. When I was younger my dad would say, 'You're young, you've got a football, just go and play football!' I would play outside all day with my three brothers throughout the summer holidays. Practising our skills, kick ups, shooting at goals, practising keeping the ball up.

Little did I know that chief scout Terry Farrell had been to watch me a few times. I never knew he had been down to watch me when I was playing for Slumberland Rangers – there were always rumoured to be scouts there so you would just take things all in your stride, you never really knew where these people were from.

Then one day I was asked whether I would like to come down to Manchester City and have a trial. Well of course I would! However with my dad always being busy and my mum being unable to drive I had no way of getting there at all. There was nobody to drop me off and nobody to pick me up. A family friend, Kevin Walker, and his son Paul, took me down to Platt Lane in those early days.

When I first went down to City I would have been 12 or 13. Between the ages of 14 and 16 when I was on schoolboy forms with the club they tried me in a whole range of positions which gives you the confidence to feel you could play anywhere. Joe Royle and Willie Donachie used to say to me when I was a professional that I could play anywhere. In the youth team set-up I actually started at centre-half.

I would play once a week at City but to get to Platt Lane without transport took planning of *Italian Job* proportions. In fact I would have been a good advert myself for GM Buses as it was then. I would have to get a bus from my house to Oldham town centre after school and then get another bus from Oldham to Manchester Piccadilly. From there I'd seek out the number 41 and head to Rusholme, getting out at the old Finglands bus depot at the corner of Platt Lane. This would be early evening.

The famous 'Toast Rack' building would be in the distance and the students would all be going out for the night, perhaps off to The International 2 to see The Stone Roses, James or one of the other great Manchester bands.

The Birch Villa pub (latterly Hardy's Well) was on the corner of Dickenson Road and always seemed to be heaving. It was a very adult world and in Manchester the pace of life was a lot quicker than in Oldham. It was OK in the summer months because it was light but in the winter it would go dark early so that's three bus rides and about two hours of travelling before I'd even kicked a ball.

In those early days I got that lift from one of my father's friends and he would run me back home but when I was 14 I had to endure this long journey on my own and not only that, I had to get all the way home again. This was an era without mobile phones. Yes there were phone boxes on the streets but they were only useful if it was working and you had some money to put in the machine!

After playing at City it would often be very dark or going dark and to be honest I was a bit scared. This was where my standard of fitness came in useful. Platt Lane was poorly lit and there were always a handful of alcoholics no matter what time of day it was hanging about the corner of Platt Fields park near the electricity sub station. I understand nothing has changed on that score even now!

So I would run as fast as I could up Platt Lane until I reached the 'safety' of Wilmslow Road and by that I mean there were more street lights. I would be in my City tracksuit but I would be paranoid about someone wanting to talk to me about football, so rather than stand at the actual bus stop I used to stand in the bushes near to the bus stop so no one would speak to me and as soon as I saw the bus approaching I would race out and appear out of nowhere and startle everybody in the bus queue! They would all look at each other and go, 'Where did he pop up from?'

Once I got back into Manchester there were more people about but then I would have to get a bus into Oldham town centre which at that time went from the Arndale bus station, later to be demolished. Back in Oldham the last bus back to near my house would have already departed which left a four-mile run to get home. I would be desperate to get home as soon as possible so what I would do is time myself with my digital watch and try and beat my previous personal best. I was always relieved to get back home but all the extra walking and running probably helped in the long run. I was naturally fit.

When you are a 15-year-old you soon realise that you need a few quid in your pocket. I saw my brothers in work and earning a few bob so I thought I'd better get stuck in. Mum said, 'Get down the market and get yourself a job.' I would walk round asking anyone and everyone if they needed a hand. Then that summer I found a bit of work at Tommyfields Market.

There was a group of lads knocking out 'Madchester'-style clothes. Baggy shirts and bell bottom jeans. Lots of people were walking round dressed in Joe Bloggs clobber, colourful t-shirts and most of the lads around Oldham were wearing Inspiral Carpets t-shirts, the popular local band.

I got a few quid packing and unpacking a van on a Saturday morning making sure the good folk of Oldham had their 'Madchester' t-shirts. During the season I would be at the ground performing ball boy duties at Maine Road. This was just before I started my apprenticeship. I never had a paper round. I never cleaned any cars. Every spare minute I had I would be out playing football, perfecting my skills. Everyone would know where I would be – just out on the field playing football.

Both my parents influenced me in different ways. There were four of us in a council house so there would always be incidents and my mum could hand out rollockings and give good advice just as much as my dad.

When it came to football – nobody forced me into it, they just let me go at my own pace. They saw I enjoyed it and realised it was something that I wanted to do. So they encouraged me.

Mum and dad came to watch me regularly for Slumberland Rangers and Terry Farrell picked me up the day we played in a final at Droylsden FC.

Terry did a great job for City but was one of the staff sacked in 1997 along with Colin Bell and Neil McNab in a big clear-out. Terry had been great for my career and when that information came into the public domain it was sad that we were washing our dirty linen in public.

These days I see friends taking their kids to football practice and I see them shouting and screaming, pushing and pushing but with me it wasn't like that.

No one said to me, 'You've got to go out and play football.' It was more something inside me which said, 'Yeah, I can do it.' I had an inner determination to do it. Nowadays you get a lot of very pushy parents, especially when there is a scout or two around from a football club. In the 1980s it was never as bad as it is now. These days parents want their kids to be footballers because of the money involved with it. Simple as that.

I think for me it was definitely about enjoyment. I had this thing for football, everything was about football for me.

By the time I was 15 I really did live for football and my whole mindset was based around ensuring that I was going to get my next contract at the club. Remember at this time there were no such things as academies in football. You would just go there for a bit of training.

I knew that the school side of things wasn't going too well. I didn't want to revise and my grades were really poor. The only thing I wanted to push myself at, that I felt motivated about, was playing football.

Instead of revising for exams I would be out at the youth club in Shaw, listening to music, playing pool and talking to the girls…usually about how I was going to be or at least hoping to be a famous footballer with Manchester City!

Daft little things stick in your memory. There was a window cleaner from round our way who was a bit of a bully. He had an English bull terrier and I was frightened to go near his house.

After a bit of egging on I would knock on his door and then run away and he'd go ballistic. I wasn't a bad lad at all but sometimes peer pressure dictated you'd hang around with the wrong crowd.

One night after going down the youth club I was waiting for the late bus from Shaw going back to Oldham with some other lads. One of them had a hammer and decided they were going to shatter all the glass in the bus shelter with it. Why? God only knows but anyway they set about the bus shelter and someone must have called the police.

I stood out on a dark night because I had a white baseball cap on and the eyewitness walking on the other side of the street was able to give the police a description of me. The other lads were wearing dark clothes so they weren't readily identifiable. I was the prime suspect, the only suspect in fact!

I was arrested and taken down to Chadderton Police Station. My mum came to pick me up. I said, 'I didn't do it mum.' She knew I hadn't done it. At the time I was waiting for my YTS contract with City. It was kind of make-or-break and if they found out about this it may have ended any chance of carrying on. As school had been a disaster, not getting a contract with City would have been a kick in the teeth and a catastrophe for me personally. There was no proof that I had done it of course. No finger prints on the hammer. No DNA, but I was scared. I went home thinking my dad was going to batter me. I had nightmares about the police coming back to the front door all the time. I had nightmares that a phone call would come from City saying, 'We are sorry, we are going to have to let you go.'

I never did find out whether anyone at City actually knew about the incident but a few days before I was due to hear about whether I would be getting a YTS contract at City I got a call from the police. The charges had been dropped. The next week I was with Terry Farrell signing a two-year deal. The date forever etched in my mind and my heart…15 July 1992.

In the months leading up to those two decisions – the possible court case and the possible contract – somehow I managed to put everything to the back of mind. Maybe they didn't know. Maybe they did. I knew I was innocent and I also knew I wanted to play for Manchester City more than anything else in the world so I just got on with it.

Looking back there's so much that could have gone right or wrong. I could have gone out and been in a fight, been out with the wrong crowd, or picked up an injury at that stage. That would have been the end of my dreams.

At school we would play in the school yard on concrete. I would be going past everyone at 100mph. I was always going at full throttle not even thinking about getting injured. I'd have run through a brick wall at the time.

Getting that YTS contract was one of the best feelings of my whole life. I was on £29.50 a week for the first year and £32.50ish for the second year. The money was irrelevant though. I was moving forward with my career. I had a chance of making it as a professional footballer and was determined to grasp this opportunity.

2

TEENAGE KICKS

AS a first-year apprentice I knew I was coming to training to learn my trade from two great full-backs in the form of Tony Book, affectionately known as Skip, and Glyn Pardoe, who holds the record for being City's youngest-ever debutant at 15 years and 314 days old, against Birmingham City.

They were the two full-backs when City cleaned up under Joe Mercer and Malcolm Allison in the late 1960s and early 70s. Now if I couldn't learn anything from those two then I'd have to seriously look at myself. Together with Terry Darracott they were my mentors as I learnt my trade.

Book had enjoyed a fairytale ending to his career when he joined the club in the late 60s, winning trophy after trophy and even being jointly named the FWA Footballer of the Year in 1969. He himself had been coached by the best in the business, Malcolm Allison, and there was probably a touch of the George Weahs about him because nobody really knew how old he was when he signed for the club! It's a bit like a woman who keeps saying she is 20-something when she in fact is well into her 30s. Youthful looks can go a long way!

Booky skippered the side to four major trophies; the league championship in 1968, the FA Cup in 1969, the League Cup in 1970 and the European Cup Winners' Cup the same season. So in 1969/70 City became the first side in the country to win a domestic and international trophy in the same season.

He was also City's manager when they won the League Cup in 1976, 2-1 against Newcastle United, which for so long had been the club's last major trophy. Peter Barnes scored City's first goal that day but the game will be best remembered for Dennis Tueart's amazing overhead kick, a memory which was all a certain generation of City fan had to cling on to.

The following season, again under Book, the club finished runners-up to all-conquering Liverpool by just one point. An own goal from the normally rock-solid Dave Watson in the draw with the eventual champions would prove to be the difference between winning and losing the league.

Skip was a man steeped in club history and had been around the place right through the years, stepping in as caretaker manager whenever chairman Peter Swales decided to press the ejector seat button in the manager's office as he invariably did in those days. A no-nonsense coach from the old school.

Manchester City were always well known for so many years for their amazing non-stop conveyor belt of talent. Ken Barnes, Jim Cassell, and Paul Power were instrumental in this and all great servants to the club. The youth team of 1986 won the FA Youth Cup and they breathed new life into a club which at the time were struggling to keep their heads above water.

The spending spree of Malcolm Allison when he was at the club second time around, coupled with signings such as Trevor Francis under John Bond and the start of the redevelopment of the main stand back at Maine Road, had eaten into the finances. This triggered off the spiral of yo-yo years in the mid-1980s, followed by the return to the top flight with the 'Boy Blues' taking on all before them in the shape of Paul Lake, Andy Hinchcliffe, David White, Ian Brightwell and Steve Redmond.

People traced the demise of City to the day Joe Mercer left for Coventry City and the day Peter Swales came in. Certainly while the signing of Steve Daley was a statement of intent, the legacy and cost of that signing would haunt the club for many years to come. Bringing the kids through was the club's only option.

Some of the press must have selective memories. It makes you laugh when you see some of the stuff they write. You would think Manchester City had never ever brought a young player through – ever! Certainly at that time if you were a young player in the north-west you would want to be on Manchester City's books. Not only did they have a great reputation for bringing kids through but so many of them went on to have good careers.

Skip would just run the bollocks off you. A very fit man indeed. Old school. Sergeant Major-like and a good disciplinarian. Sometimes he'd say, 'You don't need your boots today, you don't need a ball...just get your trainers', and we'd be off to Wythenshawe Park or doing laps around Maine Road. If he felt you were lacking fitness, he would act on it immediately and that would be his way of getting you fit. You'd run until you were sick. You'd do a run right around Wythenshawe Park from tree to tree. You'd run up the stands at Maine Road doing every single step up the Kippax. Fast laps round the pitch.

Later in my career various managers would bring in new 'specialist' fitness coaches with all these fancy methods though a lot of the message they were trying to impart simply got lost in translation. Skip would look at your attitude constantly. Did you tut, did you moan, or did you just get on with it?

You couldn't be over-sensitive around those two and you couldn't afford to take things personally. They ruled with an iron fist and it was their way or the highway.

I personally think how you handle advice is important. I gained a lot of discipline at home from my mother.

Four brothers all growing up in a council house. Looking at my friends and seeing some of the scrapes they got into. Then taking a step back and making my own decision about how to stay out of trouble and not go round challenging authority.

Lots of players who were 16 or 17 and seemingly the next big thing didn't make it because they weren't able to take constructive criticism, they didn't have it in their make-up to toe the line. With Tony Book the criticism was hard but fair. You had to take it on the chin. It was all designed to make you a stronger person.

I learned very early on to keep my head down and just get on with it and that counted in my favour. I had passed my driving test and was there at the training ground at half past eight, maybe quarter to nine. I hated being late and Tony hated anyone being late too! I was the first to arrive at training every day.

In youth dressing rooms just as in first-team dressing rooms, you'd have people who just want to get drinking, go off shagging, people who cared only about themselves. They would be filtered out for having the wrong attitude. I'd worked it out and decided very early on that I wouldn't question anything, I would just get on with what I'd been told to do. That seemed the best way to get on at a club like City. Ask no questions.

You would always learn something every day in training but firstly you had to do your jobs. As youth-team players we had a number of jobs to do; cleaning boots, sweeping up, polishing shoes, picking up the first-team kit and taking it down to Joyce in the laundry room, taking pots of tea down to the first-team dressing room, cleaning the toilets with a toothbrush, cleaning the referees' rooms or the laundry room with a loofah brush.

I'd clean the coaches' room. The players who invariably didn't make it were the ones that couldn't get on with Tony because he was so strict. I always got on with him. I grew up in a family with four kids where we all had to do our fair share of menial tasks. Four boys, and as a result my dad always had to be strict. That's maybe why I saw Skip as a bit of a father figure to me and I wasn't intimidated by him because I could relate to what he was saying and why he was saying it.

Nowadays toilets and floors get cleaned with big circular scrubbing machines. The youngsters don't even clean their own boots let alone those of the first-team squad. You've got to ask, where do they get their discipline in their lives? When we'd done our jobs in the morning we'd jog over to Platt Lane with boots in our hands, to start our day's training.

'Dinner' then was sandwiches made by Linda in the kitchen and there was also Layachi the general manager, who did a number of jobs around the club.

I always looked forward to hearing those words from Tony Book at the end of training, 'Get yourselves off home boys and see you all bright and early in the morning.'

With Skip and Glyn Pardoe it was a case of good cop bad cop. Don't get me wrong, Glyn had a hard streak as well. Skip would lay into you, take you apart in front of the others and then later Glyn would put an arm around you and say don't worry too much about this or that...just get on with things.

I always felt they were there to help you with situations. If they saw you were ready to listen and ready to work hard they would give you their time. They would both join in with training and even though they were much older than us, they were still as hard as nails, they set the bar for work-rate and expected the trainees to at least match their standards.

They ran a tight ship. Sometimes they would substitute a player and tell them to go off, get showered and changed and go home. A bit of public humiliation never did anyone any harm in their eyes.

As well as the players that have made it there were others under Skip who fell by the wayside under his tutorage who still went on to establish excellent careers elsewhere.

Neil Lennon, Paul Warhurst, Ashley Ward, John Beresford, and Michael Hughes are some. It's not just about their talent and ability, it's about application, desire, the whole package really. Nowadays everyone wears orange boots. If you wore coloured boots in those days you were a fancy dan. Sometimes things click for people later on in their careers.

At the age of 17 and on the verge of the first-team squad I was full of confidence. I was seeing a girl who was six years my senior. We were to stay together, on and off, for about nine or ten years.

I continued to live at home throughout the early part of our relationship. We never ended up living together although I got my own place in Shaw after a while. I would meet her and go out after games but my commitment was to football, certainly in those early days. She left her former boyfriend to go out with me and he never forgot or forgave me. More of him later in the book.

As I became more and more involved with the first-team set-up I kind of knew I was going to eventually take over from Andy Hill, the right-back from Bury who Peter Reid had made his first signing as manager. I had been involved with training for a while and I had been told to train hard and compete for everything. I felt I was earmarked for his position. I loved defending, I loved testing myself in one-on-ones.

There's always a hierarchy within dressing rooms wherever you go; senior players, people who have been at the club the longest. You've got to be able to handle yourself in the presence of senior players, not be intimidated by the people in front of you but also be aware of your place and be aware that you have to earn your respect.

I once told a senior player to fuck off in training when I was a nipper just starting out with the first team. I stood my ground because the player moaned about a challenge I gave even though it was fair, if robust. When the ball is there you can win it and it was a good challenge.

The player took umbrage with that and stood there screaming at me, having a right go at me and then went in to see Peter Reid about it.

They didn't like it but tough! I was just standing up for myself. I was fit and ambitious and I can't not tackle somebody just because they might not like it.

I was rugged. I wanted to break into that first team. I didn't hold back. I never thought, 'Oh there's Niall Quinn, I won't tackle him because I might get into trouble.' It was just a case of, 'This is what I am here for.'

That's why Tony Book and Glyn Pardoe liked me so much. They liked my attitude and work-rate. Their advice stood me in good stead. 'Train the way you play,' is what Booky drummed into us. In other words, don't pull out of challenges in training. It might mean you start doing it in a first-team match. Not just that but you are more likely to injure yourself when you don't go in for challenges properly.

The players and staff at the club all had Peugeot 405s from Tom Garner Motors. I remember cleaning out Peter Reid's car a couple of times and also went to the bookies on a few occasions for him as well. Reidy wasn't a particularly good tipper! Maybe he gave me a couple of tips for the nags. Sam Ellis got me to clean his shoes!

If the club could find players from the apprentice team and they were good enough you would almost certainly get your chance. I got into the team because of the good youth team structure there and the excellent coaching I received. The club were always very active at youth level when I was growing up and were seen as an example of how things should be done.

Even now, despite all the money spent on signings and wages, huge amounts are going to be poured into youth development and with the new Etihad campus going up the dream is to produce even more great young players just as they did in my day.

3

HOW WAS IT FOR YOU?

THE 1993/94 season was to be my breakthrough and I had been in and around the first-team set-up for a while. No one could have foreseen just how much of a traumatic season it would ultimately be for the club although the backdrop to it was that anything other than a positive start would light the blue touchpaper among the long-suffering supporters.

Early-season form was poor and the days of finishing in the top five, which weren't that long ago, felt an age away. The fans wanted to see some more investment and felt that the club were standing still. The FA Cup game against Tottenham Hotspur and subsequent riot from March 1993 was still hanging over everyone and with our city rivals Manchester United winning the league for the first time in 26 years our fans demanded a response.

That was City's last achievement taken away from them. Although there had been no major silverware since 1976 we could at least point to being the last Manchester club to have won the league in 1968 when we succeeded United as champions.

The supporters felt that Reidy had done a good job overall in previous seasons but we now needed significant investment in the squad to keep us competitive. Flyers had been distributed on the Kippax saying 'Keep Peter Reid but make Colin Bell no.2 instead of Sam Ellis'. The fans were looking for the team to modify their style too. Long balls were going up to Niall Quinn and tactics included our front man David White marking their centre-half out of the game and not the other way round! Defending from the front they called it.

As a relative newcomer I was excited by thinking about which players might be coming into the squad to join us. It looked like the club were busy in the Dutch market trying to do deals. We spent all summer chasing Arthur Numan from PSV Eindhoven but ended up with Alphonse Groenendijk from Ajax's reserves. A sign of City's star fading. He had been compared to Arnold Muhren because of his 'sweet left peg' but we never saw much of it at Maine Road to be fair.

In those days we were always linked with decent players; Trevor Sinclair, Brian Laudrup, Luis Figo even. Malcolm Allison, during his spell as coach at Sporting Lisbon, had recommended Figo to City in the early 1990s. City dallied and Figo went on to play for Barcelona, Real Madrid and Inter Milan, and won the small matter of 127 caps for Portugal. Even when we were being offered the best players in the world on a plate before anyone else we couldn't get it together as a club.

The first game of the season was Leeds United at home and despite a Garry Flitcroft goal we slipped to a 1-1 draw in a performance which suggested one or two extra players were definitely needed to breathe life into the squad.

The natives were getting restless. At the first away game of the season fans held up a banner in the Park End at Everton saying '£6m for players...you're a liar Swales'. In the battle between Reid and Peter Swales it was obvious who the supporters were siding with.

Peter Reid. I found him hard but fair as a manager. As a YTS player I used to clean his boots. Cleaning his car was another of my jobs. His boots, polishing his shoes for his suit after training, even going to the staff room and cleaning out the staff room.

He had Sam Ellis with him who was his assistant and who was very tough. Sam always seemed to have a stern look on his face, he would very rarely smile. You'd be lucky if you got any sort of banter or laughter out of him as he didn't really speak to a lot of the youth-team players. I think he spoke to the players he liked and the ones he didn't he never really spoke to.

Between them they seemed to have good control over the group. Reidy was quite a character in and around the dressing room. Always spoke to you, always let on and said hello first thing in the morning. There was a good blend of youth and experience in the squad at the time. We had some very good players, some seasoned players and all in all I think it was a shame when Peter and Sam both left. Looking back we never hit the high league positions again until the money came in a few years ago.

Reidy was great for me personally. He introduced me to the first team, had me training with them on different occasions and this really helped my confidence when I was around them – and also he gave me the confidence to go out and play and to try and be a better player.

You got a sense whether Peter liked you or not. I think he liked players who didn't shy away from tackles, but he also liked it when a player could demonstrate a bit of character.

Training was very serious with Reidy but it was a good environment, what you might call a workman-like environment and the place was buzzing. In training we'd play small-sided games and do a lot of work tightening up the back four.

Reidy always used to say there was no secret formula, no magic wand, success comes from hard work. The team put in a hard-working performance in a narrow 1-0 loss away to Spurs and then a home game with Blackburn Rovers, a club on the up with Jack Walker's money, meant a 2-0 win for the away side. One point from 12 and the writing was on the wall. The fans knew it and the staff knew it. Peter called everyone together and said, 'It's over, lads.'

Peter Swales brought in John Maddock, one of his mates from the papers. Maddock was known for his work for the *Daily Express* and *The People* and was also involved with one of Manchester's failed Olympic bids.

I think there was a good bit of shock around the place when Peter went because of the fact he had done so well in the previous couple of seasons. Two fifth-placed finishes were the club's highest since the late 1970s. We missed out on Europe by one point when fewer teams qualified in those days. The club were actually victims of the hangover from the Heysel Stadium disaster because fifth place would have been high enough for Europe prior to Heysel and fifth place would be good enough now.

Swales, like so many times in his failed chairmanship, pressed the panic button and he knew that if he sacked Reid the crowd would be on his back again, like so many times previously during his long reign. However the decision to bring Maddock in as a 'director of football' with the power to veto any decision made by Peter was basically just a way of sacking him indirectly. It was a charade which was to backfire on Swales spectacularly.

At that stage of my career I wasn't party to all the gossip from the first team. Certainly there would be an inner circle, a core of players like Tony Coton, Niall Quinn, Keith Curle, Steve McMahon and others… the most senior players you'd say in the squad and they would tend to keep things 'in house'.

You could feel the tension around the place though as it was inevitable that Peter Reid was going to be sacked and of course, he was, prior to the Coventry City game on the Friday night which was a 1-1 draw. There was a riot outside the ground that night as rumour swept round the ground that the new manager was inside the ground watching and his name was Brian…Brian who?

Reidy's replacement was Brian Horton who apparently had a good reputation as an up-and-coming manager at the clubs he'd led. I say apparently – I must be honest and say I hadn't heard too much about Brian Horton before he arrived at the club. In fact I hadn't heard of him at all! David Moss was to join as his assistant but to be fair they would make a good impression on the lads as a group.

I was on the verge of the first team at this stage and I was in and around the squad but Maine Road resembled a war zone and the war was being played out very publicly in the media. It was to move up a notch again shortly afterwards when former hero Franny Lee went public with his intention to buy the club and did it through the papers which angered Swales.

The week before my debut City fans demonstrated against Swales at the home game against Queens Park Rangers. 'We want Swales out…said we want Swales out' the Kippax chanted after they had a 15-minute sit-in following the win. There were crowds blocking the main entrance before and after the game and this was a sight which was to become all too familiar during my days at the club. Unhappy fans demonstrating for change outside the ground.

On Sunday 19 September Brian Horton told me I would be making my first-team debut the following night against the crazy gang of Wimbledon. What a baptism of fire for my debut – Vinny Jones, John Fashanu and the rest of them. They were good players, tough but just the sort of game you should relish. I'd been involved with the first team a few times leading up to the game to kind of give me a feel for what it was about and how the squad do things. Brian said it was the best debut that he'd ever seen from a professional footballer. It was all downhill from there Brian!

We travelled by coach in those days – no flying – and we set off the day before.

One technique some managers use is not to tell the debutant he is playing until right before kick-off, to not let nerves build.

Brian had a number of younger players at his disposal and he felt we were all ready. There were a number of injuries in the squad so it was probably only a matter of time before I got my chance.

I found the training easy. I loved running. I loved gym work and I was naturally fit. I felt ready for it. I'd been building up to this moment since the age of 12. Brian told everyone the team after our final training session and my name was casually read out along with all the others. No fuss. All he said was, 'Just prepare yourself properly for the game and you'll be all right.' He had the confidence in me that I would handle the situation in the right way.

Alan Kernaghan, our £1.6m signing from Middlesbrough and a Republic of Ireland international, arrived that week and was also in the team. His debut was in the same game.

There was no time to dwell on anything. As soon as I knew it I was standing in the tunnel and there's big John Fashanu stretching his hamstrings, with his leg up against the wall over my head, and Vinny Jones bouncing up and down like a madman and me thinking oh shit! Now the nerves had really started to kick in.

But get this. The kick-off was actually delayed – *at Wimbledon* – because of congestion at the turnstiles! I was thinking that I wanted to get through the first 15 to 20 minutes. During the game I stayed to mainly defensive duties. Wimbledon were a good, well-drilled unit with the likes of John Scales, Robbie Earle, Dean Holdsworth, Lawrie Sanchez, Warren Barton and Hans Segers. They had some household-name players and Sam Hammam, the chairman, was a legend in his own right.

You couldn't dwell too much on who you would be up against. It was more a case of how we defended. We'd practised defending as a unit all week. I don't remember much about the game, only that it was really dark, a night match, the floodlights weren't great. We conceded a scrappy goal from Robbie Earle and I wasn't particularly marauding forward a lot, we just tried to stay solid. The pitch was terrible. Bobbly and horrible. I enjoyed it a lot even though we lost. Nowadays full-backs are taught to get forward all the time but defending always comes first.

The following week I made my home debut against Oldham at Maine Road, again on a Monday night. Back in the autumn of 1993 it was a cauldron of hate inside the ground as the 'Swales out' campaign was in full swing. Some fans were staying away in protest at the regime, while those who decided to attend matches were incredibly vociferous in their criticism of the chairman and playing at right-back I could feel the venom as I moved up the right-hand side of the Kippax from the Platt Lane corner.

Meetings had taken place among the fans in Manchester and the momentum to force a change at the top was growing week by week. The fans' boycott of games at that time meant there were barely 21,000 inside the ground at that time but the passion coming down from the terraces was incredible. They wanted the chairman to step aside immediately.

It was certainly a case of having to grow up quickly. Not only was I playing during a fans' rebellion, under a new manager and alongside seasoned internationals, four of the next five games would be against top-class opposition – Arsenal away, Liverpool at home, Chelsea in the League Cup and a little matter of the derby against newly crowned champions Manchester United. The 'other' game in that run was West Ham away, hardly a stroll in the park either.

I just built up my confidence level from playing more and more games and simply keeping my place in the team on merit.

I had to grow up quickly. The Arsenal game at the Gunners' former home, Highbury, was a day I remember clearly. I walked up those marble steps thinking, 'Wow, I'm out of my depth here.'

It had been a long journey on the coach travelling with older blokes – senior pros you'd call them. Keith Curle ordering me to make him coffee. Me pretending to be asleep then him waking me up on purpose so he could ask me to brew up for him! Even if senior players talked down to you or treated you like a nobody you would have to take it on the chin in those days.

The first-team squad were all playing cards for money. In those days London trips would mean setting off at 8am and getting home late at night. There was always a culture of gambling in football right throughout my time in the game. It was just the done thing. I suppose it must have started with card schools on away trips – £50 blind, £100 blind – but by the time telephone betting came in, players, some of them good friends of mine, would be gambling and losing tens of thousands of pounds over a weekend. They would be winning thousands and then losing thousands on the very next phone call.

I suppose that's the working-class mentality with some footballers. As soon as you get the money you spend it.

Arsenal themselves had problems in their team – it was all well documented during that particular era.

So here I was, playing Arsenal and looking at the team sheet with all their fantastic players; David Seaman, Tony Adams, Paul Davis and Alan Smith, while sat in a dressing room with underfloor heating. At City the boilers had been broken for a while. Cold water only.

Arsenal won a corner and it was my job to stay on the post at corners. I recall TC – Tony Coton – telling me to stay where I was but at the same time him and Ian Wright were having a right old slanging match, TC pushing Wrighty just before the corner was delivered.

The referee stopped the play to have a word with the players and as he did Wrighty then started staring at me. I looked back at him, looked behind me, looked back at him, looked everywhere. He was trying to intimidate me and psyche me out but to be honest I hadn't really realised this was happening. I was just confused! So he shouted, 'What the fuck are you looking at!' and then I got the message – don't mess with Ian Wright!

After the corner TC just said, 'Ignore him he's only messing', and before the end of the game Wright came past me and gave me a friendly rub on the head. One of my first lessons in mind games on the pitch.

We actually had a goal disallowed from Niall Quinn, who was desperate to score against his former club, but we came away with a fighting and given the circumstances, very spirited 0-0 draw. I remember getting back on to the coach absolutely shattered thinking, 'Gosh this is what it must be like to be a professional footballer playing at the top level.' I could barely walk.

In future matches I would play at centre-half and mark Ian Wright out of the game. The Arsenal players were super fit though. They had confidence in their own ability but they were also super fit even with their well documented levels of drinking. Ray Parlour was one of the England under-21 team's fittest players and Paul Merson likewise even with his outside influences.

Next up was Liverpool at Maine Road and a 1-1 draw. They still had John Barnes and Ian Rush. They were not quite as good away from home as they were at Anfield where normally we couldn't get the ball off them. In later years we'd lose 4-0 and 6-0 there in the same week and not get the ball all game.

Going there you would fear everything about Liverpool. Walking into the place, everything is all fresh and clean and memorabilia of Liverpool's superb history is everywhere. At Maine Road it was less glamorous and we felt we could get at them. On this particular occasion it was a poor-ish game although in fact we were slightly the better team.

In my time at the club we wouldn't really fancy our chances during derby week but the November 1993 derby at Maine Road we were totally up for it and we all felt we could turn United over. They had gone out of the European Cup against Galatasaray earlier in the week, an embarrassing exit after they'd waited so long to get back into that competition and after they had baited the City fans for years for going out in the first round to Turkish opposition also, in the shape of Fenerbahce. That was the game where Malcolm Allison said that City would 'terrorise' Europe and when we drew them he didn't even have them watched.

We knew the fans expected us to win the game because we had to respond to United winning the league and there was a real buzz in training. We weren't in great form at that time but we saw the derby as a one-off match and we couldn't wait for the game because we needed to get one over on them. So for once we came out on to the pitch full of confidence.

I hated that drive to home games no matter who we were playing. I would be full of nerves. My usual pre-match meal was chicken and beans or chicken and pasta. I would be feeling sick on my journey in but as soon as I found the sanctuary of the dressing room I could immediately relax.

I was and always have been a stickler for time. I've got to be on time…I've got to be early. Getting there in good time meant you could have a read of the programme, do your last-minute jobs then whip the suit off and get your shorts on and feel ready for business.

The City fans took frozen bars of Fry's Turkish Delight in and lobbed them over the divide at the United fans.

We played really well in the first half and went in 2-0 up with two great goals from Quinny. With Niall in the side you always had a chance of something happening even if you just hit hopeful balls into the box or into the channels. He would collect them and make something of them.

At half-time not much was said and maybe that was a mistake. It was more a case of let's keep doing the same things, no talk about how to change anything should they get back into it or how we would try and keep the ball more and kill the game off. There was a feel of keep doing what we're doing and we'll win the game. Things didn't pan out that way and we ended up going backwards in the game, defending deeper and deeper.

We'd played really well in the first half but in the second half we didn't play as well and I think we stopped doing the things we were doing well. Add to that a couple of mistakes such as Michel Vonk's header straight to Eric Cantona which seemed to give them a shot in the arm confidence-wise and it suddenly became a case of us desperately trying to hang on to a 2-1 lead for the rest of the second half. We had one chance to finish them off when David White, so often United's nemesis in those days, missed a difficult chance.

I played right-back that day and most of the time I was chasing two players, Denis Irwin and Lee Sharpe. I couldn't get out of my own half to make any inroads into them. I suppose that was a difference between City and United in those days. Even if we went ahead there would be a fear, a resignation that they would just play themselves back into the game and score. The crowd felt it and the players felt it.

Losing 3-2 was a sore one. Things for me personally though were generally going well. In spite of the problems around the club I was gaining a football education at the highest level, I had made an impact and offered a solution for the club at right-back.

My performance at Arsenal away especially had earned me rave reviews and stories started appearing in the London-based national daily press.

Soon after I made my debut Brian Horton offered me a new contract. I was thrilled but just wanted a few days to discuss things with the family and get some advice. After all it was all a bit of a whirlwind. This didn't seem to go down too well with Brian.

Brian had this happy-go-lucky persona in the media but my initial impressions of him were of a very strong character and while people might think it's City, it's your club so what would you need to think about, just sign it, I'd only played a handful of games and all I wanted was just a bit of time to think it over and seek advice from people close to me.

As footballers we sign maybe two or three contracts in our career which shape the next few years. As an up-and-coming English prospect, if this was me in the present era the figures being bandied about would be comical. Hysterical. A club would understand though if a player wanted to sit down and read through his contract. In those days the power still remained with the club. They could freeze you out, make or break you.

It seemed to all be a bit of a rush. I remember coming to training probably two to three days after I'd been offered the contract and Brian stopped me outside the main entrance and pulled me to one side and told me in no uncertain terms that I should sign the contract immediately or that I wouldn't play in the first team.

This was followed by a show of strength in the treatment room by himself and his staff. I didn't know him that well at this point so I was taken aback by it all, but Tony Book was there and I grew up listening to him, and what he said always made sense. He was a reassuring figure for me and if he felt I should sign the contract immediately then maybe I should do so.

There was press talk going round at that time, Arsenal, Blackburn, there was stuff in the papers saying these clubs were willing to pay £2m for me, which I thought for someone who had only played a handful of games was laughable. I just wanted to play football as I'd only made my debut just prior to all this going on. I wasn't used to all this speculation, all this politics over contracts. It wasn't something I'd had a lot of experience with.

If you are a footballer and you are playing for 12–15 years you may have a small number of contracts to negotiate or accept during your playing career. So they are in fact key decisions in your life. In my case I had a contract when I was a YTS player which was then ripped up with this new offer. As it turned out the next time an offer of a contract would be on the table would be 1998. I would have one deal to sort now and the next time I was negotiating it was when Joe Royle was taking over and as we all know a hell of a lot happened to Manchester City between 1993 and 1998.

Each time my deals came up for negotiation I wasn't really in a position of strength so to speak. It was before the really big money came into the game. I signed the first contract for peanuts after playing just a handful of league games. I signed the second one when I was deep into the final year of my agreement, when we didn't know which league we were going to be in and after I'd been out of action with my injury for the best part of two years.

The deal I signed later with Joe started on £2,500 a week and I got £3,000 in year two, £3,500 in year three and finally £4,000 a week in the last year. The contract I signed in the Horton era really was peanuts; £1,500 a week, up from £29.50 as a YTS player. I was happy to sign though.

Personal endorsements – it was a different ball game to nowadays when whole teams might runout wearing yellow or orange boots. I managed to secure a boot deal with Asics. Sounds good eh? Think again. Just £1,000 plus three pairs of boots! Not quite the same as Ryan Giggs who was signing a lucrative deal with Reebok around about the same time.

This came about from Steve Newell, Mike Newell's brother and the marketing manager at Asics. Dave Sheron was my agent and Dave, who is Mike Sheron's brother, knew Steve and things just came about and I accepted them.

I was grateful for anything. It was better than nothing although we used to get free adidas boots from the PFA at the start of every season on account of the subscriptions we paid.

I did like cars though, that was my one extravagance. I bought a BMW 325i just after I passed my test and paid £4,000 for it at the time.

Brian Horton and David Moss had a good blend and if you did something wrong they would let you know about it, which I felt would be healthy for my career as I still needed to learn.

Tony Book and Glyn Pardoe were still about the place although Glyn was not involved in an official capacity by then but they were two great full-backs so I always had a point of reference to go back to.

Horton and Moss tried to keep the group spirits up and I thought they did quite well overall in those early difficult times. I was going to sign anyway but City were quite jumpy about it. I was a Premier League footballer but I was never on mega money at City; even when I was captain, even when George Weah was picking up whatever he was in the same team as me, my contract didn't change.

I get on fine with Brian now, no problem at all, but at the time the tactics he employed felt a bit like personal abuse. Maybe he thought it was some way of gaining respect from younger players, a way of getting them to play for him – the 'I'll show him' approach using reverse psychology. For a young lad like me it didn't work and I found it uninspiring.

What was apparent was that the spending sprees of the early 90s were over. The money had gone and Brian had to rely on some of the youngsters to fill some gaps in the squad. I think in the end that playing so many of the youngsters backfired on him.

At the time I felt we needed a bit more experience in there to help the team. The club was in turmoil and Niall Quinn, who we had been so reliant on for such a long time, was injured. What a leader Quinny was for us. He picked up a cruciate ligament injury against Sheffield Wednesday and we were lost really for goals until we brought Uwe Rosler, Paul Walsh and Peter Beagrie later in the season.

The infamous Maurizio Gaudino also came in later in the season together with another German import, Steffen Karl. Long-serving player David White felt it was time for a change and he moved on in a swap deal with Leeds, with David Rocastle coming in.

David was a tremendous addition to the squad but he did have his baggage. He was great with me, always giving great advice. You could see why he'd been such a good player at Arsenal for so long. He was about 33 when he joined us but he still had it. There were no airs and graces about Rocky, he would speak to anyone.

This was my first Christmas as a first-team professional and it was a totally new experience dealing with the sacrifice of having to play and train over the festive period at the expense of spending quality time with the family. I used to hate Christmas time, I'd always be in training on Christmas Day. I'd miss the celebrations with everyone, miss opening the presents. I had about 14 years when I would be apart from my family on Christmas day. OK, it's a great career, but we're people too and it hurts to be apart from loved ones.

We had a daft game over Christmas that year where we were 2-0 up against Ipswich Town and it was abandoned because of a waterlogged pitch. We needed those points – the one time it looked like we were going to win again it was taken away from us. We just couldn't buy a victory at that stage. Vonky had scored twice and was on a hat-trick but it counted for nothing.

My first Christmas do as a City player was a memorable one. We all piled in The Bulls Head pub which is near Piccadilly station. The theme was fancy dress. I went as Billy Bunter, the fat schoolkid. Glasses, flat cap, school uniform. A lot were dressed as superheroes but I can't quite remember who was who. Quinny I think was Batman, someone else was Robin, possibly Garry Flitcroft.

Keith Curle, being captain, had the responsibility for organising the Christmas party. These days they might go off to some swanky bar or some posh restaurant and the bill would be tens of thousands of pounds. Whatever the captain said went in those days. We would all have to go with what he suggested whether we liked it or not.

The kitty would be built up during the course of the season. Any club fines, lateness, not wearing flip-flops in the showers, any small breaches of discipline would go into the pot and the manager would hold on to the money until we needed it. Then we would all chip in £20 or whatever and lump it all in.

In those days I had only just started drinking. I was more an orange juice type of guy at that stage. We all went out literally two hours after training and guys like Quinny were serious drinkers. They could handle their drink. I was ruined after about an hour.

We stayed in there all day then went on to the drag club Foo Foo Lamarrs. We were in there until about 2am. I was walking some girl back towards Piccadilly Gardens so she could get her taxi home to Moss Side and get some food when I heard a car beep me just as we were at the traffic lights trying to cross the road. It was my best friend – and later my best man – Steve, creasing himself laughing at me dressed as Billy Bunter with some random girl on my arm. No paparazzi around in those days, just schoolfriends taking the piss then driving off!

Christmas was one of those rare occasions when all the staff would get together. The older lads would go out in their group together with trips to the races and other events. I went on a couple of trips with them as I got more established in the squad and once we went to Chester races. We would get picked up at a hotel near Kells in Hale and I would be the one player throwing up on the coach on the way back. Honestly, I was such a lightweight when it came to the booze.

City would all go to the races and no one would bat an eyelid. Football, although it was the national game, was more low profile than it was today. Plus, we weren't that good either in those days! No one gave a shit that we were there. In the main we could do what we want, say what we want, drink what we want.

On New Year's Eve 1993 we were in a hotel in Newcastle. The next day we were playing against Andy Cole, Peter Beardsley, Scott Sellars and the rest of them. There was a party going on downstairs in one of the function rooms but all the players had to stay in their rooms even though we could hear the party tunes and the screams and shouts. The other club staff would be roaming the corridors making sure everyone was playing ball but it was hard to get off to sleep with all the racket going on downstairs.

We lost at Cardiff in the League Cup at Ninian Park. The Cardiff fans were throwing golf balls into the City end. It was very intimidating. Cardiff and Millwall were probably the worst places I played at for intimidation. At Millwall you'd get racially abused running over to get the ball for a throw-in.

Keith Curle missed a penalty at Cardiff that day. I remember when he came in for £2.5m, a British record fee for a defender at the time, and £8,000 a week or whatever it was, big money at the time. He seemed to come into training in a different car every day or wearing a different watch every day!

In the second half we were playing down the slope and as we got into the last few minutes of the game it felt as if the crowd were getting closer and closer and were going to invade the pitch. The noise was intense and the missiles were raining down on to the pitch. It was as if every nutter from the valleys had turned out for this one match. It was very hostile and I was thinking 'just blow your whistle referee so we can get off' as I wasn't enjoying the experience at all.

The penalty miss meant adding Cardiff to Shrewsbury, Halifax and all the other giant-killings the club was a victim of in the bad old days.

There was already a big thing being made of the amount of time Manchester City had gone without winning a major trophy and the fans were hurting over it. Little did we know the trophy drought was only halfway through at this stage. The City fans were very strong looking back, so loyal. They kept coming through thin and thinner. If you look at the gates each weekend we were always the third or fourth highest.

Then you think about that stupid ticking banner put up at Old Trafford – with the backing of their club – which was purely designed to take the mickey out of how many years it was that City had gone without a trophy. United fans point to when they were relegated the crowds stayed with them but that was for only one season. City fans went through so much in those days and it was a bit hypocritical for United to complain about the Carlos Tevez 'Welcome To Manchester' banner when they were there giving the green light to 'official goading' of City supporters for what, ten, 15 years or more?

I found that the fans were passionate but they were frustrated too. We used to have around 100 fans come and watch us train at Platt Lane every day. We were heckled. We'd have people abuse us directly. We'd train at the far end where the dome is now.

There were the regulars who were supportive. They would want an autograph or wanted to say how well you played on a Saturday. I am sure there were players, certainly in the mid-to-late 90s, who perhaps weren't good enough to wear the City shirt and got nervous by seeing the fans stood at the side of the road stopping and watching.

I suppose with the training ground so open, this is how the rumour mill started. 'The fifth column' the media dubbed it at one point. Fans and club officials would mix freely at Platt Lane, often walking past each other on the stairs in the Oasis suite. There had always been a source of leaks. Howard Kendall alluded to it in his own book. Jimmy Frizzell went up to him and apologised for leaking stuff to Peter Gardener, a reporter at the *Manchester Evening News*. The club was too open and still a joke club under Peter Swales.

I remember the day the big Dutchman Michel Vonk came in under Peter Reid. All the other guys drove sports cars, Vonky drove a V-reg Ford Cortina. There were no airs and graces about Vonky. Built like Arnold Schwarzenegger, he was on trial at first and they put him up against Niall Quinn to see how he would get on. Fuck me, Vonky could do some damage. He was like an enforcer but a very funny lad too. In his first training session he kicked Quinny three times in the face, his boots were so high.

Sam Ellis drooled over him. Quinny used to back into players and flick the ball into channels for others to run on to but Vonky would just put his foot up and just nick it, he was good at reading the play.

The takeover which had dragged on for months finally went through after Swales was struggling to find the money to pay the Alan Kernaghan transfer fee and Franny Lee, much to the delight of the City faithful, replaced him. They were selling 'Spot On Franny' t-shirts outside the ground celebrating his success from the penalty spot when he was a City player with the nickname of 'Lee Won Pen'. Franny had returned and in his first game in a carnival atmosphere we beat Ipswich again in the rearranged game.

We were then thumped 4-0 at Coventry and you'd see the papers and you'd think Brian Horton was about to be sacked. We were slipping into a relegation battle and the media compared what was happening now to the top-five finishes under Reidy.

Around March we couldn't buy a goal and we weren't winning our home games. The fresh faces that came in at this time though gave us a much needed goal threat. We tried to sign Anders Limpar from Arsenal but he chose Everton and we ended up with Peter Beagrie. What a good signing he turned out to be though. We also signed Uwe Rosler and Paul Walsh who, despite already being about 35 years old when we signed him, was fit as a fiddle and gave us another way of playing.

Later on he would give Quinny a new lease of life by feeding off his flick-ons and his intelligent running would create that little bit more room for Niall. Adding that extra bit of experience in the final third of the season probably kept us up.

I remember the day Uwe breezed through the door. He had built up a reputation in his own country which had only recently been re-united. Uwe had been an East German international.

He mooched in looking like someone out of the German rock band Scorpions with his long hair. His accent meant he sounded very abrupt but he always meant well and he soon settled in. He worked his socks off in training and really helped some of our younger players.

Uwe got a ticking off early on in his City career. All players reporting for first-team duty had to wear a suit, a shirt and a tie. Up pops Uwe with his black Uhlsport rollerneck. We used to rip him mercilessly for his taste in clothes or rather his lack of taste!

We would follow him around shouting 'UHL-SPORT' and he was like someone with Tourette's in reply, 'YOU…FARCKK ORFF, FACK YOO, FARCKK OFF!'

Uwe soon hit it off with Walshie and together they formed an incredible partnership. They kind of knew exactly where the other one was at all times.

We escaped relegation with a couple of late wins and were safe by the time of the Chelsea game which was the last time the Kippax was open as a terrace. The heart and soul of the club was going to be difficult to replace.

I never had the opportunity to stand on the Kippax as a fan and I kind of regret that. As a boy I would go in the main stand and if I was involved with the squad but not part of the team I would usually sit in the main stand too. I would sometimes run up and down the Kippax steps if we trained inside the stadium. I remember Monday mornings we might do that and there was still all the rubbish left over on the floor and you wondered what it must have been like to be part of this great mass of people.

In April 2014 it was the 20th anniversary of the standing going at City and that Chelsea game and the City fans did a Kippax tribute with lots of tickertape and daft inflatables during the game against West Bromwich Albion. You'll never take the Kippax. The spirit lives on.

At the end of the season I made my debut for England B and look at the players who played in that game; Warren Barton, Dean Holdsworth, Rob Lee, Paul Merson, Chris Sutton, Chris Armstrong. The Premier League had quality English players in depth. Could we even put out a B team these days ?

I was also then called up for the England under-21 team for the Toulon tournament. England were led by Kevin Keegan and Dave Sexton. My room-mate was Bruce Dyer. I got on well with Kevin Keegan in those days but little did I know that our paths would cross later in my career.

There was very little freedom there for the players. Just training, eating, sleeping and a bit of card school in the hotel; £50 here, £50 there.

Forty minutes or so round the pool because it was red hot there in the south of France. No mad sunbathing. No internet in those days and in truth not a lot of fun. It was not an enjoyable trip but I made friends with the likes of Chris Bart-Williams, Robbie Fowler and Dominic Matteo.

It is probably worth putting on record here that we won the tournament! We beat Portugal 2-0 in the final and Chris Makin took my place as I had picked up an injury. That was also the fourth time in five years that England had won the tournament so we were crowned champions again at a time when there was pressure on us as a group to deliver.

I learnt that a tournament is as much about how well you travel and how well you handle the little things as much as some of the football you play on the park.

I made my England under-21 debut at Brentford's Griffin Park in a 1-0 win over Denmark. During that particular era I was playing regularly with a lot of great players, for example Michael Oakes, who is Alan Oakes's son of course. He was on Aston Villa's books at the time before he ended up at Wolves.

Sol Campbell, Ray Parlour, Jamie Redknapp, Nicky Barmby, Julien Joachim, Chris Sutton, still at Norwich then before his move to Blackburn to pair up with Alan Shearer (the original SAS striking partnership), Chris Bart-Williams, Trevor Sinclair, Dean Gordon, Bruce Dyer, Robbie Fowler; the list goes on.

We never really got a chance to express ourselves as characters on the Toulon trip as we were mainly stuck in our rooms. Bruce Dyer is a born-again Christian now, a great lad but he had his problems when he was younger, he was crackers, mental and he helped pass the long hours away.

The set-up was centred around getting players who would go on to play for the full national team accustomed to tournament football and the travelling and the preparation in between matches.

If you look back through the record books, in those days we won it practically every year. There were more English-born players to choose from in the top flight too.

I remember the two lads from Leeds, Jamie Forrester and Kevin Sharp. There was a bit of publicity about these two having gone from the FA School of Excellence to Auxerre in France and then back to the Premier League. They were great characters but sadly for those two, their careers didn't hit the heights some predicted.

I played in the first game but then picked up a niggly ankle injury and had to sit out a few days. With me missing training sessions I never got a look-in again during that tournament.

There was always good banter flying around with the under-21s at meal times and for all the self-discipline we had to show, I enjoyed being part of the set-up and it was a privilege to be selected to represent my country.

So my first season as a Premier League player had passed and what a learning curve that was. I felt proud to play for City. We were treading water in the league but it was my club and I was enjoying playing for them.

4

SOME MIGHT SAY, WE WILL FIND A BRIGHTER DAY

AFTER the Toulon tournament and a short summer holiday, my next bit of football was City's pre-season trip to the Isle of Man. City were playing my hometown club Oldham Athletic among others.

These days City jet off round the world; America, China, Hong Kong or somewhere like that to showcase the club to the worldwide fan base we now have. I knew lads who went to City who felt a trip to the Isle of Man was the nearest we were going to get to playing in Europe!

When you think about the the Isle of Man you might think of the TT races or perhaps Snaefell, the mountain which is the highest point on the island and a place where you can see England, Scotland, Wales and Ireland all from the same spot. There you go. There's that Europe thing again.

I have got to say that as a player who didn't consider himself to be one of the senior players at that time I was pretty well behaved. I stayed in the hotel, didn't go out on the lash, didn't go out to the clubs and drink with the fans. However in terms of our recent history the trip is worth a mention because the fans really enjoyed that venture even though we didn't cover ourselves in glory on the pitch.

It kind of illustrated what sort of a club and whereabouts we were at that time in our history. Invites from Barcelona for pre-season friendlies must have got lost in the post around then.

I remember the actual game against Oldham. We lost 3-0 with about 50 Oldham fans and 3,000 City fans in a ramshackle old ground. The City fans were treating it like a stag do in Spain, they were really letting their hair down.

People were having their own races round the athletics track while the game was taking place. They were nicking the corner flags. They were showing what great fans they were, with their self-deprecating humour. They can laugh at themselves, the City supporters, they don't take themselves too seriously unlike some other sets of fans I could care to mention.

In those days the chant 'We never win at home and we never win away' really meant something.

I can't quite remember exactly who was on the tour but normally you'd have the likes of Peter Beagrie, Andy Dibble, Uwe Rosler, Niall Quinn and Steve Lomas who might go out and socialise with the fans. Some of the players came back to the hotel with various stories after some of them had been in a nightclub socialising with all the supporters.

People had been walking naked across zebra crossings during a thunderstorm. Other fans had fallen asleep drunk in bus shelters. Just madness. These days there is less interaction between fans and players at all Premier League clubs which is a bit of a shame really.

Uwe Rosler. A cult hero and the fans loved him. They loved his goal celebrations and they loved his energy and commitment. It took the East German quite a while to settle in to the club fully but everyone in the dressing room was really supportive of him. After 9,000 of them had sung his name to the 'Go West' tune on the last day of the previous season at Sheffield Wednesday, he bonded with the fans even more on this trip even though he still managed to pack his trusty black Uhlsport rollerneck even for this trip. The lads slaughtered him for that.

You've seen how well he has done in the game in management, coming back to the Etihad to knock City out of the FA Cup with Wigan Athletic in 2014. He shows no fear and he went on record once to say he wants to be City manager one day in the future. He has even named his sons Colin and Tony after Colin Bell and Tony Book! These days I think he likes drinking red wine but fair play to him, he would buy beers for the City fans and they loved him for it.

Niall Quinn's disco pants are the best. They go up from his arse to his chest. They are better than Adam and the Ants. Niall Quinn's disco pants. This song started during City's pre-season trip to Italy back in 1992. Niall had a fight with Steve McMahon and the Irishman came off the better after their altercation and was feeling rather pleased with himself.

Inside the nightclub later on McMahon ripped off Quinny's t-shirt and Niall, who was ever so slightly the worse for wear, was prancing about bare-chested along with Rick Holden (who had only just signed). Quinny had some cut-off denims on and a group of resourceful Blues were in the same club that evening and sung it that night then consequently took it back to the Kippax with them.

So the song was born. Our song, not Sunderland's I might add, and the song of choice that night in the clubs of the Isle of

Man. Everywhere by all accounts was rocking to the sound of this particular terrace anthem!

Andy Dibble, a big character with a big heart, always seemed to have a female fan club following him around! Dibs would come in to training sometimes with a whiff of garlic and booze on him. You'd then see him with a bin bag trying to sweat it all off.

One time he had some blood pressure problems and the club doctor, Dr Luft, told him to take a few days off and ordered him to have complete rest. The very next evening Tony Book caught him out in Altrincham with a cigar in one hand and a bottle of wine in the other. I guess that's just how footballers used to relax in those days.

Peter Beagrie was always full of chat and banter and never one to shirk giving an opinion. Beags would always have a good one-liner up his sleeve. No surprise to see he is doing so well with his job on Sky Sports.

Terry Phelan was my room-mate at the time and he too was a very confident guy. Phelo and Curley had come in from Wimbledon where their flamboyant chairman Sam Hammam had worked miracles keeping them in the Premier League.

I think the idea of putting me and Terry together on away trips was to put us two full-backs in the same space so we would bond and develop an even greater understanding.

Terry was a fitness freak. He used to have a set routine of doing loads of press-ups and sit-ups in his room before having a shower. Phelo liked a good night's sleep. Once he was ready to drop off that was it. The telly had to go off. Even if I wanted to watch something I had no chance, the telly was going off! Terry gave me lots of great advice in those early days and was a good influence on my career.

Terry was a kind of big brother for me at that time and when I see him now there's still a mutual respect there. Tony Coton is another one. He watches City in the boxes. He's been in the lounges at the Etihad and still gives me the biggest bear hugs you can imagine.

Tony is still one of the best keepers I have ever worked on a football field with. The fans turned on him a little towards the end with the move he made but that wasn't his fault. The club were in the situation where they needed the money after rebuilding the Kippax. Eike Immel came in and forced him out of the team but who was the better keeper? TC all day long in my eyes.

I think there might have been one game where Phelan and Beagrie had a massive row in the bath. It could have been Arsenal away. Incidents like that were very few and far between though.

People always talk about 'typical City' and if there was ever a season to illustrate this then 1994/95 was just that.

Just look at some of the results in this particular season. United away, lost 5-0. Tottenham at home, won 5-2. QPR away in the League Cup, won 4-3. Southampton at home, drew 3-3. Liverpool at home, won 2-1 just after they'd won the League Cup. Blackburn away, a truly remarkable 3-2 win where we also had two goals disallowed against the team that would go on to become the league champions.

I played in all of those games bar the Southampton one. It would be a pivotal season for the club – weren't they all back then? – but with hindsight the changes that would take place at the end of the season would ultimately make things much harder all round for everyone.

The background was that it was the first full season of the new Franny Lee regime. The club had lost the old Kippax Street stand, a major source of income, and it was a time of great change off the park. Money which would have gone on players had to go on rebuilding the stadium. It was a strange sight seeing Maine Road with three just sides and no Kippax. Slowly but surely the new Kippax stand was rebuilt as the season went on.

Mick Hucknall once sang that 'Money's too tight to mention'. This seemed to be the case at City – the purse strings were tight even after the takeover and with four clubs to face relegation at the end of this season with the Premier League changing from a 22-team league to 20, it was absolutely imperative we stayed in the top flight. Of course the fans had higher expectations than that but as the season went on we found ourselves being dragged into the danger zone more and more and just staying up in the top flight began to represent a realistic ambition.

Brian Horton wanted to play progressive football but it was being done on a shoestring. To play the way he wanted to play, in a 4-2-4 system, you really needed to have the players to pull that off.

Nicky Summerbee was the only addition that summer and we'd lost David Rocastle, Mike Sheron and Steve McMahon, three players who had between them clocked up hundreds of top-flight games. In the cases of Rocky and Macca maybe that was the start of higher wage-earners being let go.

Training under Brian would be a lot of eight-a-sides on a three-quarter pitch. It was all about possession really. How to win the ball back when the opposition had it. How to keep the ball when you had it. Playing two-touch or three-touch on a full-size training pitch to encourage people to move it quicker all the time. I found training enjoyable. Horton himself had probably learned a few tricks from David Pleat at Luton Town.

The famous old Maine Road pitch was widened and with Peter Beagrie hugging the touchline on the left and Nicky Summerbee on the right, the expectation was of flowing football and a throwback to the days of Tony Coleman and Mike Summerbee, part of the famous front five in the late 1960s with Neil Young, Franny Lee and Colin Bell making up the quintet.

We were actually sixth at one point in early December but we simply couldn't sustain it. We didn't have the squad to do it. The thing about our system was that the wingers didn't tuck in, they kind of stayed wide which was quite brave.

We finished 17th after a relegation battle. We had certainly changed the way we played since the Peter Reid era but the results were very up and down. We could have finished a respectable 11th had we beaten QPR on the last day of the season but we fell away after that tremendous win against Blackburn late on.

Looking back now this was probably one of my most consistent seasons as a player. I was still on a massive learning curve but my physical attributes were growing and the more I played the more composed I felt on the ball, with both feet. I had good pace. People commented that I had natural ability and was able to make things look easy even when running at full tilt.

The fans saw us as rivals to United and not just in a geographical sense either. They had high hopes after the Franny Lee takeover but for me it was about keeping my feet on the ground, progressing my career and really establishing myself in the City side.

I had nudged my way into the England under-21 set-up already and with another season of progress under my belt who knew where I could have been heading.

Going back over some of those games, perhaps the one which was the most talked-about that year was the 5-2 victory against Spurs. All the media were raving about our movement that day. It was a great advert for the Premier League in a game which was broadcast all around the world.

I remember looking forward to testing myself against Spurs. It was the early days of the Premier League and they were one of the first clubs to start importing lots of foreign talent. With Jurgen Klinsmann, Ilie Dumitrescu, Gica Popescu and the likes of Teddy Sheringham and Nick Barmby they boasted a great forward line.

Later that season in the return game at White Hart Lane I played at centre-half and I remember marking Klinsmann. Even in the first five minutes his movement was just unbelievable. He was big, strong, powerful, always on the move, disguising his runs and he was very sharp indeed.

That 5-2 game was a pleasure to play in. Like Spurs, we too had our forwards creating space and we all played with a lot of freedom. Beags and Walshie would always be positive in their play. We'd use our width to isolate the opposition full-backs then open the opposition up.

Peter Reid was more successful results-wise than Brian Horton and Reidy's game was all about discipline. Even though I'm a defender and my job is to bring about a clean sheet I'd still prefer to play in a game where we win 5-2 than trying to grind out a boring 1-0.

This was also a game where some of our young guys, Garry Flitcroft and Steve Lomas, started to get national recognition.

Looking back at the early-season form that campaign we seemed to do well at Maine Road and not so well away from home. We were full of goals but shipping a few too many by the time we played United away. It's simply amazing to think of the derby game these days and the way City can just turn up at Old Trafford and get a result, beat them 6-1, whatever. I remember the derby game on 10 November 1994 at Old Trafford for all the wrong reasons. It was a tough night for the club where we found ourselves on the end of a 5-0 hiding. It kind of highlighted where both clubs were at that particular time and in which direction they were both heading. The gap was growing year on year and as City players we were aware of that.

United had been trounced 4-0 in Barcelona the week before and the City fans brought Barcelona flags to the game. The media were expecting a United backlash and for them to take their frustrations out on someone.

They always say derby matches were supposed to be great levellers but it wasn't a level playing field when we had to play them in those days. Supposedly one team could be top and one team could be bottom and it would be close and even though we had made a decent start to the season overall, United had more ammo than us in those days. Add to that the usual paltry allocation for City fans and it really was a case of going into the lions' den.

With the Franny Lee revolution now fully under way the City fans hoped of recreating those glory days from the 1960s and 70s when a trip to Old Trafford simply meant a bus ride and maximum points. In the league between 1962 and 1976 City won seven, drew one and lost just one derby match at Old Trafford. So even though on paper you've got no chance, as a City player going there in those days we still had something to live up to – our past – and you still had the expectation levels from our fans demanding that we get a result.

I had the small matter of marking Ryan Giggs in this game at a time in his career when he was lightning quick. Tony Book had jokingly said to me before the game, 'Remember, he can't run without his legs!'

Now remember these were the days when you could still put a challenge in and try and win the ball through tackling. Skip was not advocating that I 'do' him, merely that I let him know I was there.

Other players literally got away with kicking an opponent out of the game but I wasn't a dirty player. I thought of myself as very quick and I loved to defend, take the attackers away from the goal area and show them the corner flag so for me marking someone like Giggs was the ultimate challenge.

We went into the game as huge underdogs but I was determined to test myself against a player of his ability. I remember going in for a tackle with him and went to win the ball and unfortunately I caught him on the ankle and he ended up going off with an injury.

I actually had a good game that night and people commented on that afterwards. They had Andrei Kanchelskis at his peak on the other side and there was no respite as they brought Paul Scholes on as substitute for Giggs. Kanchelskis was running riot on the other side against Terry Phelan, who was no slouch himself.

With injuries in our goalkeeping department we had Simon Tracey playing for us that night and it would be one that none of us would ever forget. Least of all Brian Horton. It was the start of the fans cooling towards him slightly.

We'd actually started the game quite well and Garry Flitcroft could have put us in front before they scored their first. At 1-0 we were still in the game but they got one right on the stroke of half-time and then got a third just after the break.

I think we only knew how to play one way. Normally a team three down would think about damage limitation but we kept on pushing our wingers forward which naturally left gaps for their players to exploit. Not just that but every little thing went for them that night, every clearance went to them, every deflection went to one of their players. It was just one of those nights.

After they'd scored the last goal on the breakaway from our corner I remember Mark Hughes chasing me round just after we'd kicked off again, saying 'you're fucking useless you' and I thought to myself, 'Yeah, at 5-0 down I must be useless!' Maybe there were derbies where we played worse as a team but they just seemed to put all their chances away on that night.

It's a very different build-up to the derby games now. Forget Fergie's 'not in my lifetime' nonsense, City are the star attraction in town now but in those days everyone expected United to win comfortably each time and we would go into the games over there – especially lining up in the tunnel – thinking we would probably get beaten. We were kind of beaten mentally before kick-off.

Peter Schmeichel, Gary Pallister, Denis Irwin, Ryan Giggs, Lee Sharpe, Andrei Kanchelskis, Mark Hughes, Paul Ince, Roy Keane; we simply didn't have the team to match them. Apart from that game where we were 2-0 up at half-time, we never went into the games thinking we were going to get too much out of them, so tactics and how we were going to deal with them just went out of the window in the build-up. It was just a case of let's give it a go and see what happens.

At the end of the day, how do you deal with many good players? I think it's fair to say we as City players had a bit of an inferiority complex in those days, even if the supporters never had one.

It was 5-0. We couldn't get away from it. I used to read the papers and see what they said about things but that all stopped for a bit the night we were trounced in the borough of Trafford. I couldn't even go out of the house. I was so embarrassed. We all were. We were all affected by it.

I would go to training then go straight home. That would be it for about three weeks afterwards. I didn't see anyone, didn't do anything. I never saw any of my mates for weeks. Never returned any of their calls. My poor mum, I didn't even see her. She would come to the house I had in Shaw, clean up a bit while I was out training, but I couldn't even be bothered ringing her back to thank her. Sorry mum!

I would normally go out on a Saturday evening after a game but I didn't want to have any conversations with supporters. I just stayed in and thought about things. I was just so embarrassed. It was just the absolute shame of it all. What was amazing though was everyone used to say the only positive from that night was my performance and I felt terrible about it all! Christ knows how Simon Tracey must have been feeling.

I was never on the winning team in a derby in those days which was very disappointing when you look back. I even lost in Ken Barnes's testimonial game in May 1992 when I managed to get a start with the first team.

It is a big difference to these days where City go into the game as favourites against United whether it is at the Etihad or at Old Trafford.

Just to illustrate my point about the papers, another thing I noticed around this time was the way they, specifically the *Manchester Evening News*, wrote about you and wrote about the team. Most City fans thought it had a bias towards United and called it the 'MUEN' but when I was starting out Paul Hince was the City reporter and he was a big blue and of course a former player. Paul got a few games in the 1960s in the famous era of Lee, Bell and Summerbee.

Hincey was a winger and played in the 1967/68 title-winning season although sadly for him, he didn't play enough games to be able to pick up a medal. He then went on to play for Charlton Athletic.

Around the same time as I started making my way into the first team the *Evening News* started giving players marks out of ten for their performances. I am reliably informed that when his sports editor told him to start giving the players marks, Hince himself seemed put off by it and thought the players might turn on him.

The first time he did it, on a City pre-season tour of Italy, he waited outside the team dressing room and asked the players if they would give themselves a mark out of ten and he would go with that – just to show them if you like that the mark he was giving didn't mean that much to him and so that way none of the players could accuse him of having a personal dig at him if he gave them a low mark.

However I think I was bothered about Paul Hince and the marks he gave because in those days the main coverage you would get about Manchester City would be in the *Manchester Evening News* so the only in-depth verdict people could read was usually in that paper. OK, there would be Piccadilly Radio and GMR as it was in those days with their phone-ins but as for the written press it was the *Evening News*. Everyone in Manchester read it or was aware of it.

There was no talkSPORT and no BBC Radio 5 Live. Even programmes which came out later such as *You're On Sky Sports* with Rob McCaffrey or Gary Newbon only tended to focus on whoever was at the top of the league.

I used to be baffled by the marks I would get. A lot of us were. It would be the talk of the dressing room at times, a source of amusement among the lads and some extra mickey-taking just when you didn't need it. I thought I played badly sometimes and would get an eight. Then other times I thought I had a great game and would get a five. I used to think, 'Has he been to the same game as me today?'

It wasn't just the scores though. They then started putting a comment with the score underneath about your contribution to the game. This was discussed as well in the dressing room and we found some of the comments ridiculous at times.

I suppose when things are going against you – and let's face it, we were in decline during the 1990s – the comments would hurt. They would be an irritation. It's bad enough you've lost the game but sometimes you saw it and could have a laugh and joke about it – brush it off. At other times it would really get under your skin.

Come to think of it no one ever used it as a motivational tool. Perhaps they should have done actually but no one pinned an article up on the board in my time at the club and said, 'There, prove them wrong.'

We were aware of the reports though and after a while you couldn't even pick up the papers because you were that scared of what was going to be in there. Especially if they included comments from the supporters.

The 1994/95 season was very up and down for the club – mostly up before Christmas and mostly down after it but for me personally I felt I was progressing. Young players need to play regularly in order to progress and I was getting first-team football. I was now the established right-back for Manchester City Football Club.

We hadn't won a trophy since 1976 but we still had our fair share of 'celebrity' fans. Oasis were by now just about the biggest band in the world and Noel and Liam Gallagher would never be too far away from the reception area or the executive suites, especially if it was one of the London away games.

Both of them love the club but I found Noel wanted to talk with you more about the game than Liam did. Noel would want to stay and ask questions about things that had happened during the match but Liam would just be waving his arms about to get attention, shouting and storming off, making a scene.

Eddie Large was a big friend of Roy Bailey's so Roy invited Eddie in and asked the lads to welcome him. He only ever came in a couple of times but back in the 1970s he used to sit on the bench and crack a few jokes!

Now and again he'd bring his sidekick Syd Little along with him. One time he came into the dressing room at a game when we were 3-0 up and the players relaxed so much they ended up drawing 3-3. That was City all over. This was the Bournemouth game in 1989 when Ian Bishop was pulling the strings for the Cherries.

Soon after the derby with United where we were 2-0 up and lost 3-2 we played Sheffield Wednesday and lost 3-1 at home. Bernard Manning was in the dressing room beforehand with his grandson I think and going round taking the piss out of everybody one by one, 'This one here, the man with the big nose [Michel Vonk] he is the man who cost us the derby last week.'

Again, not the most professional of set-ups where Premier League players are being taken apart by fans in their own dressing room minutes before going out to play.

Even though I was a Premier League footballer I would still be expected to muck in with special events and occasions. We were very much a family-orientated club and the Junior Blues pantomime at the City Social Club would be an occasion where everyone would come together. It was one of the highlights of the calendar in many ways.

There's many a City fan out there who was brought up on Sunday mornings of Gary Megson or Ian Brightwell in fancy dress singing daft songs to a room full of kids. I had a great many friends at the Junior Blues – Ian Niven, Jessie Ward, Geoff Durbin. With far fewer permanent members of staff working at the club everyone knew each other.

As players we had rotas. First-teamers and youth players all had to attend Junior Blues now and again. Even if you'd been out at 6am down Wilmslow Road on a Saturday night/Sunday morning you had to sober up and attend. We were the only club doing that sort of thing and the Junior Blues had clocked up a membership of 37,000 during its 25 years in existence and at one time was the biggest junior supporters' club anywhere in the country.

People look at the good crowds City got during the bad days and asked why the fans stuck with the club. Why did the crowds hold up? They were in the relegation zone and heading for the third tier and still getting the fourth highest crowd of the weekend. You used to see experts on television debating it, as if there was some psychological explanation needed. They were just local people supporting their local club!

They were people who in the main had parents and grandparents who were Blues and they carried on the family tradition and joined the Junior Blues as a result. It was just what you did. Manchester people always supported City even in the bad times but in my time people always used to say, 'What would this club be like if it fulfilled its potential?' Well, we are seeing interest in the club go through the roof now.

I received a call-up for an England get-together with Terry Venables and got to train alongside the cream of the country's talent. When I turned up there my jaw hit the floor. Alan Shearer, Paul Gascoigne, Les Ferdinand, David Platt, David Batty, Tony Adams, Stuart Pearce, Darren Anderton, they were all there.

Euro 96 was still a while off but at that time I was still ahead of the likes of Gary Neville. I suppose there was Rob Jones and Warren Barton around as competition but my agent said to me, keep doing what you're doing and you'll be all right. Being a Blue there would always be something just around the corner though to bring you straight back down to earth...and there was!

The very next week I was on duty at Maine Road. We had a monthly luncheon club and it was my turn to meet and greet the guests. I parked up in the car park behind the Platt Lane End. By now I had a 3 series BMW convertible. A group of lads approached me asking me if they could have a ride in the car, ten or 12 of them, surrounding me. 'No way' I thought and put the car keys down my underpants and walked towards the main entrance.

Halfway through this luncheon I was asked to come to the main entrance. The security guard walked me over to my car, which had been completely trashed. Slashed tyres, broken windscreens. Back down to earth with a bump. Even when you were being considered as a possible England player of the future it was still a hard life being a Blue!

There were some interesting characters from the Moss Side area who used to target me and I think it was this lot who did this to my car. I had to be careful where I went at times. One time I was in Henry's Bar having something to eat just minding my own and I ended up being chased down Deansgate by lads looking to rob me and shouting, 'We're gonna shoot you!'

It didn't stop me going out in town though. Not at all. Who wouldn't want to be going out in Manchester in the mid-1990s? I was a Premier League footballer enjoying my football and enjoying my life. I wasn't seeking fame but had worked hard to earn a contract and my place in the team.

Footballers have to sacrifice a lot to actually make it to the top. Win or lose, after a game, why wouldn't I let my hair down on a Saturday night? It's different now though, it's straight in the ice bath then hydrate yourself and rest! We usually played on a Saturday at 3pm in those days so you could go out on a Saturday night and the feeling was that you could have realistic recovery time before the next game or the next heavy training session.

These days with so many varied kick-off times – Saturdays, Sundays, Mondays – the players couldn't go out for a knees-up even if they wanted to.

I only went to the Hacienda once and I didn't like it. I found it seedy and moody. I went to Sankeys and I went to The Boardwalk. At this time Manchester still had some clubland left and it was just before it went all café bar culture with the likes of Mash and Air, Bar 38 and those types of places popping up. If I had to pick one favourite spot looking back it would have to be The Boardwalk which was run by that 'honorary Mancunian' Dave Haslam.

I would drag some team-mates down and I'd see players from other teams in there too. Michael Thomas, the man who won the league for Arsenal so famously in 1989, used to go in there a lot during his Liverpool days. It was a heady mix of hardened clubbers, general party people, wannabees and gangsters. The bouncers on the door were big Blues and used to look out for me. Charlie who was on the door of The Parkside worked there. Many Blues will know who I am talking about.

Sometimes I would be pulled to one side before going in and be tipped off about who was in there. So and so from Salford. So and so from Cheetham Hill. I always felt a bit embarrassed about jumping the queue but sometimes I would take a couple of mates and they just loved it!

We would vary where we went in order to avoid trouble. Sometimes successfully, other times not so. We'd go in Loaf in Deansgate Locks. We'd go to the gay village. I'd go to lock-in ragga nights in Moss Side but I would also go to places like Mr Smith's in Warrington, or Discotheque Royales on Peter Street, full of cheesy music and slappers! You could say I had an eclectic taste in music. Or maybe I was just a party animal.

I was a regular visitor to the famous Easter Bloc record store on Oldham Street and I'd often bump into Andy Cole browsing through the vinyl in there. I used to know DJ Leaky Fresh quite well. He had his own show on Sunset Radio in those days. I just got to know all types of people. Nutters even. Sometimes in life you feel that you need to have that element of protection close by.

City weren't the number one team in Manchester back then but we were still Premier League players and therefore a target for certain people. I used to get anonymous phone calls at times, 'We know where you live and we're going to come in and rob you.'

I was friends with Pat Barrett, the boxer, and he had lots of boxer mates. Often I'd be out somewhere and one of these new friends would be in the same place and let on to me so I knew that someone would be keeping an eye out for me. It was weird being in the public eye but I never went looking for trouble and would have been quite happy just keeping myself to myself. I was out in Hale one night and saw Roy Keane sat in the corner of the same pub, wearing a dufflecoat and necking pints. You see, it affects different people in different ways.

Whatever genre of music you were into you could find it in Manchester. Going off the various styles of clobber and haircuts all over the ground you could tell the punters were all into vastly differing types of music but the one thing that brought them together was their love of Manchester City.

You'd go over to take a throw-in and make eye contact with people who had probably just picked themselves of the floor and dragged themselves to the match after attending an all-night rave or something.

You had that indie crowd who would be clinging on to that 'Madchester' sound going in 5th Avenue, 42nd Street or do the crawl from the Lass o' Gowrie to The Old Garratt and then end up in The Conti Club, The Granby or The Brickhouse. You had another crowd, more into dance music that would start in Atlas or Dry and end up in the Hacienda.

Lots of people in Manchester would know someone in a band. If you were a lad in Manchester and you didn't want to be a footballer the chances are you would want to be in a band. Oasis came on to the scene. Big Blues. Match-going Blues who wore their hearts on their sleeves. They were happy to tell the national media that they were City fans when others wouldn't own up to it. I can recall them coming on to the pitch a few times at Maine Road in those days and Liam especially giving the v-sign to opposition fans.

I wasn't the only City player to have problems. Steve Lomas and Jeff Whitley got on the wrong side of people after a night out in the Fantasy Bar. One of the doormen pushed Jeff into the road and threatened him. What I got to find out was that certain places had links to certain gangs in Manchester and it was in your best interests not to cross these guys.

Players like Niall Quinn had no trouble. Sure he would pop in places like The Salutation on the outskirts of town but players who lived in the south Manchester/north Cheshire belt tended to avoid town and go out in those areas. They never seemed to experience the same problems we did. To be fair, when I stayed out of town and went to places out of the way like Benny's in Radcliffe I never had any problems. You have to be choosy where you go out sometimes.

Back on the pitch the league form was dipping. We went out of both cups, 4-0 at Crystal Palace and 3-1 at Newcastle United, and even the home form began to suffer.

For me personally though my career was on the up and 1994/95 was a season where I played some of my best and most consistent football in a Manchester City shirt. I was pitting my wits against the best wingers out there; David Ginola, Andy Sinton, Trevor Sinclair, Ryan Giggs. I would say David Ginola would be my most difficult opponent of all time.

By Easter we were deep in the mire. You looked around the dressing room and saw real quality there, the nucleus of a side that had finished in the top five a couple of years previously. So I felt eventually we would get out of it but the longer you go without a win it becomes difficult mentally. You do feel the pressure.

The chairman would occasionally come into the dressing room and say things to the players and there was one time after a game when he came in and had a pop at everyone and when he'd gone a couple of the senior players commented that maybe they should have stood up and said something to him at the time. Wimbledon away after a bad defeat was one such occasion.

It wasn't just poor results. There were some poor performances in there too but you get that over a long, hard season. The Premier League doesn't provide any easy games.

It all seemed to change around Easter though. Things just clicked. The result against Liverpool came out of absolutely nowhere. Cult hero Maurizio Gaudino popped up with a late winner meaning we went into the Blackburn game with renewed confidence.

Blackburn away. What an absolute cracker that was. Uwe and Paul Walsh were among the scorers that night and what a partnership they had now developed. Their goals were a big part in keeping us up that year. Uwe scored 22 goals that season and by now the fans were declaring undying love for him by wearing 'Rosler's Granddad bombed Old Trafford' t-shirts around Maine Road.

That night against the eventual champions I was up against the likes of Alan Shearer, Chris Sutton, Stuart Ripley and Jason Wilcox. Afterwards Kenny Dalglish on Sky Sports commented, 'Where have City been all season when they can play like that?'

That result and especially performance proved that on our day we could give anyone a game.

After the match Brian Horton took the cheers of the crowd and there was much backslapping taking place. He felt he had done enough to keep his job. We all did. Well, we did for about half an hour. On the way back home we stopped off at the Haydock Park Hotel. It was there that we found out from the manager that he would be moving on at the end of the season. Apparently he had just been told by the chairman. Looking back I think the timing was disappointing. It certainly took the shine off things and we didn't win another game that season.

Paul Walsh was a terrific little player for us who gave us absolutely everything. His movement was superb. People always talk about his partnership with Uwe but he played off Niall Quinn too and it was great for Quinny at the time to have Walshie there because his runs were so intelligent it gave Niall a bit more time on the ball and Quinny always had a pass on when he received it.

QPR away in the league was one such example of his terrier-like work-rate. He chased down a back-pass and the keeper's clearance went straight to him but he kept his composure and scored. A goal out of nothing, a 2-1 win when our away form wasn't great. That was also a game where we had nine men as both myself and Andy Dibble ended up getting our marching orders. So we must have had a bit of character in that team. The chairman obviously felt he wanted to make a change though.

John Burridge got into the side towards the end of the season. He was a big character and a big personality. He'd walk around the dressing room in his slippers. He'd do daft things like stand there juggling oranges and apples. A complete one-off. Some games we'd have Beagrie doing somersaults on the wing and Budgie doing a handstand on the touchline!

Steve McMahon. I had a lot of time for Macca. I found him to be a nice fella. He'd give you rollockings, he'd give you praise, he'd give you advice but he'd won leagues and had a wealth of experience. Not only that, but he kept an eye out for us younger lads too. Advice from people like him was invaluable so you would take it on board.

When the results started to slip and the pressure was on him I feel that perhaps Brian might have found it easier to pick a fight with some of the younger lads like me rather than some of the older pros. I think he had to keep them onside so to speak.

These days I get on get fine with Brian, absolutely fine, but in those days I didn't warm to his management style. You'd walk past Brian in the corridor and he couldn't walk past you without saying something to wind you up. The longer he was in the job, the more he seemed to be feeling the pressure, such was the weight of expectation on him. That job, with all the baggage that comes with it, had been the downfall of managers with far bigger reputations than Brian.

When we won games that season he seemed happy to take the credit. When we lost the emphasis seemed to go on to the 'kids'. Perhaps that was an easy way out. Or was it simply a way of getting us to improve and shape up? We felt we were being blamed when results went against us; the likes of me, Garry Flitcroft, Steve Lomas, John Foster, Rae Ingram, David Brightwell. Maybe it was easier to highlight the weaknesses in the games of younger players than tackle the attitude of some of the senior pros. Who knows? He did keep picking me though.

After one press conference where these comments came out again Macca took matters into his own hands and had a strong word with Brian, saying, 'Leave these lads alone.'

The 1994/95 season was remembered as one of daring and attacking football from Manchester City, moving the ball quicker with wingers hugging the touchline, but the club still generally seemed to be slipping further away from the top. We never really had a settled defence and at times we were very open. You can see from the goals in the 5-0 defeat at United how open at the back we were, especially against counter-attacking football.

After the Blackburn win we felt we'd done enough but the news that there was to be a change affected the dressing room. Form petered out and that was a shame because all of us – players, management and supporters – had been through it that season. The financial situation had not gone away and finishing higher might have made the club an extra few quid which they needed at the time.

We felt that some kind of cull would be on its way in the summer but the decision had already been made and Franny Lee decided to replace Horton with somebody new. As it turned out that would eventually be our famous World Cup winner Alan Ball, but initially there was a vacuum at the club as we had a few weeks where for whatever reason we weren't able to attract a manager.

Perhaps word had got out across the football world about how things were going at the club. Alan Ball the following season would prove to be even more testing for all of us. One thing is for sure, Brian Horton wasn't well known by the City fans before he came to City but he was afterwards. He did a good job in the circumstances. He certainly didn't get time but looking at the Premier League nowadays nothing really seems to change on that score does it?

5

AND AFTER ALL, YOU'RE MY ALAN BALL

'OH for fuck's sake, not that squeaky-voiced twat Alan Ball!' Yes, I can vividly remember the reaction from some of my team-mates when they heard that Alan Ball was going to be appointed as our new manager.

Now that particular reaction came from our wing wizard Peter Beagrie. I recall that Niall Quinn wasn't too impressed either. As players you need to feel the club is heading in the right direction. This appointment lacked any inspiration as far as many of the players were concerned and the supporters made their feelings clear about it in the local media, saying it was a ridiculous appointment.

They still backed him, with their own variation of Oasis's anthem 'Wonderwall' which went, 'I said maybe, you're gonna be the one that saves me...and after all, you're my Alan Ball.'

OK, maybe not enough to win an Ivor Novello award but a decent effort from the Blue Army. Not many people felt Ball was going to save the club though, in fact, his appointment was the catalyst for years of misery.

On his first day at training, his wife was upstairs at Platt Lane waving his World Cup medal to anyone who cared. Nobody did much. His wife would often be at the training ground. Ball tried to stamp his authority but having her flashing his medal about like Tessa Sanderson at the Olympic Games did nothing to help his cause.

We had 25 or so players. All looking for leadership, all seeking assurance; 25 different characters, lads, all different in their own right looking for someone to come in and control the dressing room. Looking for someone to come in and recognise the different personalities within the dressing room and work with us all to get the best out of us. Someone to direct us, show us which way we were heading that season.

City fans remind me of a pre-season game up at Hearts where we lost 5-1. About 2,000 Blues went up there and they ended up all walking out in disgust. A crisis of confidence set in among the support. We drew the first game at home to Spurs and we were lucky to get anything out of that and then lost the next eight in the league so we were as good as down by the autumn. One of those matches was Newcastle away where I was sent off. Paul Walsh had gone and Gerry Creaney had come in.

We were played off the park in that first game but clung on for a point. We couldn't retain possession. The clever running off the ball and attacking intent of the Horton era had evaporated already. A team scared to go forward. It had all fallen apart. We were a laughing stock. We were changing managers every other season and look where it had got us. The players felt for the fans, certainly at that time. The fan base stayed loyal and continued to back everyone at the club. There was no leadership though.

Alan Ball had come in and he was Franny's Lee's appointment. He was a good friend of Franny's with the pair having played together for England and having links to Bolton Wanderers.

I think he came in with the intention and with the backing of Lee that he would get rid of some of the higher-paid older players who were there at the time.

I remember one training session early in his reign we put on a keep-ball session. It was a Monday morning, the pitch wasn't the best at the time – it was quite warm and dusty – and all the lads had been out on the razzle over the weekend and we were straight into training.

The likes of Dibs, Keith Curle, Terry Phelan, Peter Beagrie and Niall Quinn were together, a few of the older lads, and we tried to keep the ball for 15 minutes. I don't think we strung more than three passes together. It got to the stage where it was so bad it was laughable, a few players broke down in tears at how bad this session had become and after about 20 minutes Ball lost his rag with us all and decided to send us in and for us to come back at 1pm, around two and a half hours later.

Ball blew his top – effing and blinding, 'You lot are an absolute fucking disgrace, you can't keep the ball for more than three or four passes.' Telling players to come back later on didn't go down too well with a few of the senior pros and I remember walking off thinking, 'This is the first time I've seen anything like this, ever. I'm not sure what's going to happen here.'

As the lads were walking off a few of the older lads were saying, 'We're not fucking coming back at 1pm, no chance', and I recall cars screeching out of the car park. There was a total lack of discipline across the club from top to bottom. Me being a young lad at the time, I was sat in the dressing room with my kit on, just trying to keep warm. I was thinking, 'Well I need to get back out at 1pm – I can't drive home!'

Some of the squad had raced to get their clothes, put them in the car and then stormed out. You could see the strain and tension building in the group and on this day it just exploded. They were already sick of Ball.

Some of the older players felt that Ball was only brought in to ship some of them out and in the end they were proved right. Tony Coton, Garry Flitcroft and Paul Walsh were just three of the players moved on that season. Flitcroft was sold towards the end of the season for £3.2m and we bought four players to replace him with money to spare. The squad was getting bigger but the quality was dropping.

This of course was the season that Georgi Kinkladze came in. Franny Lee walked this fresh-faced lad on to the training ground while we were in the middle of an 11-a-side game.

The lads just thought it was some kind of wind-up at first. Here was this overweight guy with a mop top haircut covering half his face and no one had seen or heard of him before.

Alan Ball stopped the training session and said, 'Lads, this is Georgi. He doesn't speak a lot of English', then put him in one of the teams. Gio didn't touch the ball for a few minutes so Bally stopped it again and said, this time to Stevie Lomas, 'Right, next time you get the ball just give it to him.'

Anyway Lomie finally released the ball to him and everyone's jaws just hit the floor. Picking up the ball, Gio ghosted past two or three players then dropped his shoulder, of course he had this knack of feinting one way and then he'd go the other way, losing players without even moving the ball, just a drop of the shoulder. It was just an unbelievable thing to see.

At the end of that training session we were doing some fitness work and we were doing laps around the pitch. Georgi took part but after the first lap he decided that was enough for him and decided he was going to jog the rest of the way! So while the rest of the squad were doing 60-second laps he was casually trailing behind everyone else. It was funny seeing that but what an extraordinary player he turned out to be.

At that time we had a lot of players in the squad whose game was simply about closing people down and working hard. They didn't have that gift that Georgi was born with.

He made his debut in that opener against Spurs and showed a few glimpses of magic but the work-rate of the opposition players would often catch him out.

He had an unbelievable left foot and could see a pass that probably most of us would never ever see in our lifetimes.

In the time he was there he was a good lad and I got on really well with him. After a while he got to understand slang and the lads' sense of humour, chipping in with his own brand of banter once he knew a bit more English. This was actually just a few swear words he'd picked up after hanging around with Nicky Summerbee for a while!

Gio was a good player to have in the squad at that time, certainly as an option to have because he was so different to most other players in the Premier League. He was probably the most individual player on City's books since the days of Kaziu Deyna.

Looking back at the goals he scored at that time, the Southampton goal for instance – goal of the season on *Match of the Day* – they take your breath away. One up at Middlesbrough comes to mind too where he waltzed through the entire defence. And the last-minute goal against Aston Villa. I threw the ball to Niall Quinn, who with his back to goal, played Georgi in and he fired home a late winner which brought half of the North Stand on to the pitch.

Gio was gaining sharpness and match-fitness and by now starting to contribute – but really only when he had the ball.

When he had the ball you could liken him to Diego Maradona. He had the ability to be one of the best players in the world. There were some games that season where he dragged us through at times. If he didn't have the ball though, he had no work-rate and he went into hiding a little. He wasn't the only one though, there were others that season who would go missing.

However it should be remembered it was November moving into December by now and almost halfway through the season. Yes, things were starting to show some signs of improvement. Bizarrely, Alan Ball actually won the Manager of the Month award for November which in itself was usually a curse. It was to be a short-lived period of respite though and for myself, the fixture the week following that Villa game turned out to be life-changing for me personally.

It was Leeds United at Elland Road, always a tasty fixture. Leeds had been champions of England only three years previously. It was a big game and for once we had some momentum going into it. It was another great win for the team, 1-0 with a goal from Gerry Creaney, who was actually the substitute who came on for me.

It was however to be a life-changing afternoon for me personally, a day when I became scarred both on the inside and the outside and you find out for yourself, you just don't know what's around the corner when you are a footballer. A day when your hopes and dreams can shatter and evaporate in a split second.

We were in good nick going into that Leeds game. We were on a run and despite the obvious faults of the manager, we had regained a bit of confidence and felt we could get something out of the game.

It was 0-0 in the first half when it happened. Nothing much of any note had happened in the game up until that point. Both sides had been feeling their way into the game, trying to win the midfield battle.

I was pushing forward down the right and I clearly recall the tackle from Mark Ford which damaged me for such a long time. I remember stepping away from him, trying to block him off and shield the ball. He slid around the back of me and caught the right side of my knee, sending me flying up in the air. My shoulder hit the ground before my feet did. The impact was so forceful that my knee ended up going in the total opposite direction to the rest of my leg. My body went to the left and my knee veered off to the right.

I tried to get up but couldn't put any weight on my leg. Everything had seized up and I was aware of the knee which now seemed to be pointing to the side. My kneecap didn't seem to be where it should be. My foot also seemed to be veering off at a tangent.

I slumped back down again full of fear and waited for Roy Bailey, the physio, to come on to the pitch. I was immediately stretchered off to some applause. I knew I wouldn't be going back out on to the pitch again that afternoon but, sat in the physio's room shortly afterwards, it hadn't dawned on me just how bad things really were.

I was given painkillers, Roy packed my knee with ice and both him and Ronnie Evans tried their best to comfort me. Roy had to stay with the rest of the first team for the duration of the game and then immediately after the game he told me I was to be taken to the Bupa hospital in Whalley Range. I was absolutely devastated with what was happening. I simply couldn't take it all in. I was trussed up in the back of an ambulance and rushed back to Manchester.

Ford went to Burnley and I played against him in the 1998/99 season. He played in the 6-0 game when we thumped them at

Turf Moor. Ford has never said anything about the incident to me. Looking at the tackle now it was a bad one. A really bad tackle from behind and these days there would have had a long ban for it.

For all the macho image of football, this is your livelihood, everything you've worked hard for over many years to get to this place and to suddenly realise you are the victim of a career-threatening injury is very hard to take. The pain was getting worse and worse. Throbbing, searing pain, taking me over. The painkillers kicked in then and I was completely out of it.

I had a girlfriend at the time but I was still living at home so my mum and dad had been contacted during the match and told where to come as I had been injured. When I came round it was in the hospital and it was reassuring to see them both sitting at the end of the bed in that hospital.

I was only 24 at the time of the injury and up to that point I didn't really think about a lot else other than playing my football. That happy-go-lucky demeanour I had evaporated instantly when I was told that realistically there was an 85 per cent probability rate that I would not play again. You won't be surprised to hear that I took that news very badly.

I had a 'scope' put down, a tiny camera inserted into the knee to see what sort of damage had been done there. I was told I had completely ruptured my anterior cruciate ligament. I had damaged my medial ligament as well. I was heartbroken. All you want to do is play football. I'd known nothing else since the age of 12 really.

Eventually the plan was to let the swelling go down and give the knee a chance to settle and see exactly what kind of damage had been done and formulate a plan from there. It would be a waiting game. I couldn't have imagined there and then that it would be 21 months in total that I would be out of the first team – with various setbacks to endure along the way.

In those days clubs weren't required to have chartered physios, even in the Premier League, so I couldn't get the help I wanted, the help I needed.

Just into the new year, January 1996, one of the most promising players in City's history, my pal Paul Lake, announced his retirement. It goes without saying what a tragedy it was for him and he spoke so well in his book about everything he had to go through. A brave man and a real gentleman and the City fans love and respect him with genuine affection right to this day.

The most naturally gifted player at the club robbed of fulfilling his potential. I remember first getting to know Lakey when Peter Reid was the manager. We were at the playing fields at the University of Manchester training grounds in Northenden doing some fitness work with Tony Book. Walking, jogging, running, walking, jogging, running again, then a practice game. We'd all be breathing hard and taking in drinks.

Lakey would have done the running with so much ease, he'd just be carrying on running and he'd be wearing a knee brace at the time. I'd played against Lakey in training sometimes and I knew just what a good player he was.

I remember speaking to Lakey about all the operations he'd been through and asked for advice. Paul tried to guide me on how to make various decisions including who should operate on me, 'Don't accept the first thing the club may say to you, get some different opinions, try and get the best treatment you can even if the suggestion comes from another source. Don't let the club force you into going to see their surgeons and people they suggested to there may be a better option available.'

Lakey's advice was invaluable. How I should take my time over this and think about what kind of operation I should have and how the club should look after me after I have had the operation.

He mentioned someone in Cambridge called Dr David Dandy who if I remember correctly wasn't actually a knee surgeon, he was an ankle surgeon. Dr Dandy had helped Dean Saunders, the former Liverpool, Aston Villa and Derby County striker, to recover. Saunders was one of the first players to make a full recovery from an anterior cruciate ligament injury. He had operated on Alan Shearer who had come out well from it too.

I think I was taking a bit of a risk but it was a calculated one. Based on Lakey's advice I decided I should pay him a visit because he had such a good reputation for reconstruction and as well as Lakey there had been some other excellent recommendations about his work to go off.

My leg was still in a knee brace at this time but I still ended up travelling by car down to Cambridge all by myself – the club provided me with an automatic vehicle.

The team were playing down south somewhere that day so Roy Bailey came across to meet me to attend my very first meeting with Dr Dandy, which I found reassuring. It was a hotel a stone's throw away from the clinic he normally practises at.

When I got there I was told I'd have to wait for another month to see if we could plan the operation.

Dr Dandy explained he needed things to settle down further so he could determine the full extent of the damage and see exactly what he was dealing with.

So he just told me I'd need to give the knee another month's rest to help it settle down a bit because there was still a lot of trauma around it, a lot had happened to that part of the body and I would need to come back for another evaluation when the time was right.

He said he would need to put another scope in there so he could decide what would be required. Dr Dandy said to come back in another month and let the swelling go down in the meantime.

I went back as he said and at this following appointment he agreed he would arrange the booking of the operation. So then we waited for a few more weeks and after that I was down in Cambridge once again, but this time Dr Dandy confirmed that he himself would be operating on me.

Sitting up in my hospital bed the night before the operation I was full of fear. I was thinking the worst – what if this operation doesn't work? What if this is the end of my career as a professional footballer? Obviously having listened to Paul's account of going to America and seeing different surgeons and having so many operations then trying to understand both the mental and physical anguish he had to put up with, it was a case of sitting there with this nauseating feeling of dread hanging over me. Even if it went well I would have a long long way still to go.

I was a player who used to get up and down the pitch, get tackles in, chase and harry people and if I couldn't do that then what use would I be to anyone?

Up until this point it hadn't dawned on me fully just how important this operation was going to be. I hadn't contemplated what would happen if it didn't work.

I vividly remember waking up after the operation and being in absolute agony. I had a drip in my knee with morphine pumping into it and it was the most horrendous feeling. I didn't feel I was actually there, I just felt that I was lying somewhere… somewhere and very injured.

After the operation I was told I wasn't allowed out of the hospital until I could walk a flight of stairs. I managed to do that just a couple of days after I had the operation.

I remember having the drip pulled out of the side of my knee and the pain was worse than anything I'd ever felt, having this tube tugged out of the side of my knee.

For weeks after the operation I was still pumped full of morphine, painkillers and stuff like that. I'd be sat upstairs at Platt Lane – it was the only place I knew where to go in the morning. The lads would be traipsing in and there I'd be, just sat there with my crutches on the table in absolute agony mentally, watching them come upstairs for a drink and a piece of toast, watching them get changed and then they're all going outside to start their warm-up, leaving me all alone gazing out of the window at them all. I felt crushed. Useless. I'm sat there on my own, feeling sorry for myself, and I used to get very upset about it.

To feel like such a spare part when all the other lads go out for training, that mental anguish was almost unbearable. It's just the way it is that when you are not available to play and to train you are probably viewed as being of no use, of no value whatsoever. Your self-esteem plummets. It's hard to explain to people. Other footballers would understand. You go from being at the peak of your powers to being on the sidelines.

I was in a cast and a leg brace and there was plenty of pain associated with that. As I was hobbling round people were walking past me tapping me on the shoulder saying, 'Are you alright Edgie?' and I was just nodding back unconvincingly.

Being around the place wasn't doing me any good at all and Roy Bailey suggested it might be best to continue with the rehabilitation well away from the club. Seeing the lads go out training impacted on me the hardest and I think hurt more than anything else.

Now I am quite a strong character with deep reserves of inner strength and determination but even I sank a bit towards depression. Having everything you want to do in life taken away from you, in one tackle, can be hard to take. You have that special feeling when you run out of the tunnel at Maine Road and feel the buzz of the crowd, and to not have that anymore was extremely difficult to deal with.

People make a great play of the sums of money players earn. We're only human beings though. We still have feelings. At that time I wasn't earning amazing money. In fact I never really did earn amazing money. All I wanted to do was play for the club that I'd been at from the age of 12. I found it really difficult to understand why it had happened and how I was going to get back to the player I was beforehand.

During that time, I could have easily drifted into a world of drink, drugs and prolonged severe depression. If it wasn't for my strong family unit I might have gone off the rails. At times like this you realise that family is everything.

I was getting big hearty Sunday dinners at my mum's; roast beef, rice, potatoes, carrots, the lot. It sounds like nothing much but the point is I had people looking after me, making sure I had a normal routine.

It was a family tradition really. All of my brothers would come round, bringing their wives and their kids. At least I had that normalness to tap into, the security of a strong family unit around me which helped me make sure I kept my feet firmly on the ground.

There were times, in those early days especially, when I couldn't speak much at the dinner table. It was good to be around loved ones but I didn't have much to offer in the way of riveting conversation.

During those weeks immediately following my exploratory operation I just walked around in a daze. I had a knee brace on and I didn't really want to do anything at all. I didn't want to go out. I became a recluse. Just sort of sat at home every day with my foot up on a stool.

I had a few visitors. Some of the players came to see me and Franny Lee visited too, telling my parents I was a £4m player and I would be back sooner or later which was just what I needed to hear at the time. He phoned my mum and dad and reassured them the club would do everything in their power to help me back to full fitness.

I gave an interview to *City Magazine* while I was out, saying I couldn't believe how bad daytime television was! The way it was done it was designed to come across that I was doing OK and coping mentally with it all but deep down it was a lonely time.

My mum used to hover round me, asking if I wanted a cup of tea every five minutes and eventually I just ignored her. I was so bored with it all. Nothing would have made me happy. Also I was bottling all my feelings up and storing resentment and anger. I am sorry that my mum had to see that side of me but inside it was a nightmare time for me.

There was the odd occasion where I had to get out of the house for my own sanity. It took me a long time to talk to my girlfriend and immediate family about how I was feeling about it all. I kept a strong lid on my emotions. I felt no one could possibly understand what I was going through so there was no point really in trying to explain to anyone how I was feeling. I had some good lifelong friends around me at the time who cared about me and said come on, lets go out and have a few drinks, help you unwind.

So go out we did and I'd sit there with a knee brace on, going out with five or six of my mates who'd look after me really well and give me some release from being in the house. They would also see I made it home OK.

There was this one time though when I had just popped out without my group of friends. I went out to a pub in Oldham with a knee brace on and got attacked by a group of local numpties, some of whom were armed with knuckle dusters. I was sat there minding my own business in the corner but then out of the corner of my eye I saw this group came in.

I told you earlier about the girlfriend I had who was six years older than me and the boyfriend who couldn't get over being dumped. This group were linked to all that. I noticed them come in but was sat away from them. I carried on quietly in the corner but instinct told me that something might happen. When I got up to leave one of them hit me.

Another time I was threatened with being taken up to the moors and 'dealt with'. Charming. I kicked myself for being in the wrong place at the wrong time and for being so stupid to have put myself in that situation.

These days you go to Carrington and it's a different world to what we had. It's just unbelievable how pampered the current squad are. There are lots of player liaison staff looking after their every need plus also they get advice that we never got; advice on how to handle yourself in public, where to go, how to handle idiots who have a go at you, which I think is absolutely fantastic.

I was a local lad. I'd go out into Manchester but I would also stay close to my roots. Oldham is a small town and perhaps people knew where I tended to go on a regular basis and where they felt they could run into me if they went there often enough.

They would have seen I was on crutches and not able to walk properly or fully defend myself yet they still went out of their way to have a go at me. At the time it really was the last thing I needed.

Being injured and then watching *Match of the Day* and football on the box generally I would find utterly depressing.

Unless you go and see a psychiatrist you can't open up about how you feel about something like that and unless you've been in that position where your career is in the balance you can't really explain it and talk about it.

People ask you if you are OK and it's difficult to say, 'No I'm not.' You can't say no because people might start thinking you are a soft touch or a bit of a mental case. You are public property being a City player and you feel you have to constantly be polite all the time to everyone or just say what you think people want to hear you say.

Paul Lake had said himself that you tend to bottle a lot of these things up and look inwardly because it is difficult to let people know how you are feeling. You become your own best friend and completely reliant on yourself.

So it was a lonely time but towards the end of the season and with the club fighting for their lives in the drop zone I went to a few games in a friend's box in the Platt Lane stand to cheer the boys on as best as I could.

Watching these matches among the fans, as a supporter, was nerve-wracking. We had shown a bit of spirit and gone down fighting in the home derby which we lost 3-2. Uwe Rosler scored an equaliser then pointed at the name on his shirt. He then ran right over to the dugouts and had a right go at Alan Ball.

Then there was Liverpool on the last day of the season. It was bad enough I'd played in the two defeats in four days to them back in September, 4-0 in the League Cup and 6-0 in the Premier League.

The equation was not simple on that last day. Despite a couple of narrow 1-0 victories in previous games at home to Sheffield Wednesday and away at Aston Villa, both Coventry and Southampton had matched our results meaning we were still in the bottom three at kick-off. We were relying on other results. Even a win might not have been enough. However we could still stay up with a draw should other results go for us. Typical City.

The status of me as a footballer was in the hands of my team-mates. They would determine whether I would still be a Premier League footballer in 90 minutes' time.

Peter Swales had said after relegation in 1987 that the club would never be relegated again in his lifetime. The former chairman passed away in the week of the Liverpool game and maybe that promise died with him. If we were to be relegated now it would be under the Franny Lee regime. There was a sombre minute's silence before the game. Two years previously, the Forward With Franny campaign had swept Peter Swales out of the boardroom after so many years of underachievement. The City fans didn't like Swales but they still gave him his moment of respect.

Relegation wasn't supposed to be part of the new revolution. It would be absolutely disastrous, especially with the cost of the new Kippax to consider and the potential loss of the Sky money. Many supporters who had witnessed Luton Town's David Pleat dance on our grave in 1983 were present again on this occasion. As the crowd fell silent to remember Peter Swales we thought, 'Would the outcome be any different though?'

As well as ourselves, Wimbledon, Sheffield Wednesday, Coventry and Southampton were all in danger.

After the silence there was a massive roar of expectancy but then the players simply froze on the day and early on we were 2-0 down with Ian Rush, who had scored so many goals against City, celebrating with extra vigour as he could see a Mancunian team heading towards the drop.

There were just 20 minutes to go and it was still 2-0. Suddenly out of nowhere we got a penalty and Uwe put it away for 2-1. Then Kit Symons stayed forward and managed to bag an equaliser.

The whole ground was going absolutely berserk. The fans were full of hope once again. Just one more goal. Only football can do this. Only City can do this. Heart in your mouth stuff.

Everton came from two down to beat Wimbledon 3-2 and stay up in similar circumstances a couple of years earlier. The supporters would be hysterical if we could get that third.

Then cheers rang round the stadium. Was there a goal elsewhere? No, it was a false alarm. No one told Alan Ball though who instructed Steve Lomas to keep the ball near the corner flag. After a few minutes Niall Quinn had to tell Ball to change the tactics. We had lost the momentum we had. Liverpool were on the ropes and we wasted five precious minutes in the meantime.

The final whistle went. The results came through from elsewhere over the public address system and the reality sank in. The Liverpool fans cheered. I wonder if they would have taken it at Anfield had the boot been on the other foot and our fans did that.

I was sat in the box in the Platt Lane end looking down on the pitch after the Liverpool game on that hot and sunny afternoon. We had run out of time and the fans were in despair. Relegated. Bewilderment. Disbelief.

I was still injured and forced to watch my Premier League dream disappear before my eyes. Sitting there watching my team go down just like all the fans in the ground did was heartbreaking. I was injured and could do nothing about it.

'Don't look back in anger', Noel Gallagher famously once sang, but it was hard not to when you looked back at that season, both on a personal level and for the state of the club, now relegated for the third time in 13 years. We had taken one solitary point from the first 30 and it had been the equivalent of climbing Mount Everest ever since.

Niall Quinn had to face the media. 'No one told me there would be days like this in football,' he said on *Match of the Day* that night.

Earlier in the season Alan Ball had been playing Kinkladze when he was plainly not match fit. The more experienced players in the squad tried to give an opinion at the time but were overlooked.

It's healthy for the older players to have a degree of influence in my eyes but Ball would not listen to anyone. Guys like him were just so far up their own backsides it was impossible to be heard by him. He'd be shouting one thing on the touchline while his assistant would be shouting something totally different. Give it to Georgi, that was our only tactic at times. You do your job…then give it to Georgi.

'Alan Ball's a football genius' the fans sang. Even he must have known it was tongue in cheek.

City would bounce back though. That was the opinion of Ball who pointed to the fact that if you took away those first ten games, the points total gathered indicated we weren't one of the three worst teams in the league. We were actually ninth on form across the final 28 league games!

We would be the biggest team in the Nationwide League and the crowd would stay as loyal as ever. Everyone would be back here again in August raring to go. All soundbites to tug at the heartstrings of supporters who would be expected to dig deep, forgive and forget yet again. There was no Arab takeover on the horizon at that time. Not even a sniff of a Shinawatra.

For me personally though, I had no idea what the new season would bring. I was still nowhere near making a recovery.

6

WE'RE NOT REALLY HERE

THE summer of 1996 and a pre-season trip to Ireland was where the City fans' anthem 'We're not really here' took off. Opposition fans will have heard this song and may have wondered what on Earth this song is all about.

There had been various theories as to how and why this song developed. One version was that the club's hooligan firm, the Guvnors, sang it after sneaking in at Luton Town in the late 1980s when there were no away fans supposedly allowed. Another version was that it was the story of City's rollercoaster ride through the divisions and that the fans couldn't believe what was happening. Neither are true.

The actual explanation is that it was about a City fan from the Prestwich and Whitefield Supporters' Club who passed away after a weekend in Amsterdam a couple of years prior to this trip. His friends from this branch were singing the full version of it in Ireland and others joined in during a boozy pre-season. It then carried on to the away games and then to home matches.

The full lyrics are, 'If you're drunk you will die, if you're sober you will die, so it's better to be drunk than be sober when you die, just like the fans of the invisible man, we're not really here.'

You could say I was the invisible man at this stage. Out of pre-season and nowhere near the first team.

I simply couldn't comprehend what had happened to me. It just felt that my knee was of no use to me anymore. Not even halfway through 21 months of sheer agony and at this stage I hadn't had all of my operations during that time. I was a forgotten man and the club had their own crisis developing on the pitch.

That song mentions drinking and the fans who bought season tickets again and would turn up at away grounds in their droves began to hit the booze as watching City became a 'day out'. Being a Blue in those days wasn't about glory. It was about being there and keeping the good name of the club going.

Some of the players we had on our books at that time weren't right for the club and couldn't handle the pressure of playing in front of so many fans each week with that expectation level that the club had to bounce back to the Premier League. No wonder so many of the players also turned to drink.

Alan Ball had remained unpopular – no surprise there – and after a defeat at Stoke City at the old Victoria Ground, where the home fans joined the 7,000 travelling Blues in a chorus of 'We want Ball out' the manager was relieved of his duties just three games into the new season.

Franny Lee was in the tunnel the following Monday and came in with Ball, clearly quite emotional that he'd had to sack his friend. Or had Ball 'resigned'? Either way Franny was not best pleased. 'You fucking bastards have got this man the sack! I hope you're proud of yourselves!' he raged as Bally looked down at the floor crestfallen, a broken man.

Asa Hartford was offered the job permanently but politely refused, although he did take control of team affairs for the home game against Charlton Athletic where in a frantic finish a last-minute winner from Gerry Creaney lifted the gloom but even then Hartford still didn't want to take over.

He was in charge the following Saturday against Barnsley, who would eventually go up to the Premier League as First Division runners-up. This was my mate Jeff Whitley's full debut and his suicidal back-pass gifted Barnsley's Clint Marcelle a winner.

Three defeats from the first five games. Everyone knew the season was already falling apart. All the hype and bluster from Ball had just been papering over the cracks but no City fan had bought it anyway. There was a win at Port Vale before a defeat at Crystal Palace with City still unable to attract a manager to the club. 'Nobody's blue and white army' sang the City faithful. 'Nowhere…City are going nowhere' was the reply from the Palace fans.

The papers seemed sure that George Graham was coming in but he was talking to Leeds at the same time and from the outside it looked like City were just his back-up plan and he was using the club to strengthen his position when negotiating a big fat contract with the Yorkshire club.

Then it was going to be Howard Wilkinson. He won the league with Leeds in 1992 and was maybe still seen as a 'big name' by some of the supporters. The London press ran scurrilous articles hinting that any prospective manager might not get things all his own way at the club. 'Don't take any fanny from Franny' was one particularly memorable headline.

Steve Coppell eventually came in but only stayed for a month. I didn't really have too much to do with him, I only spoke to him just the once because I was out injured, so that whole episode surrounding his short-lived reign was a bit of a mystery.

There were a lot of rumours about the reason for his departure. Some of them have gone down in City fan folklore. All I can say for fact is that the job was a very big job at the time and he wasn't the first manager to quit the hotseat at Maine Road. He did have the full support of the fans though and when he left everyone was bewildered. They had even briefly adapted the 'Wonderwall' song to him. 'And after all...you're my Steve Copp-ell.'

Phil Neal had come in as his number two and soon commented that watching City was 'the best laxative in the land'. He seemed to suggest to the board after one win that they should back him or sack him. They sacked him.

It was a circus. We were just staggering from manager to manager, and we had so many players coming in – and on big money too – it was hard to keep track.

Nigel Clough came across from Liverpool and he didn't play that many games, yet at the time was one of the highest-paid players on our books.

The whole club just descended into a bit of a farce and we became a laughing stock at that time. The players were part of the problem but they felt it too.

Dave Bassett, or 'Harry' as he was nicknamed, was the latest in a series of managers to be linked with the job and then go on to publicly turn it down. The humiliation of seeing the club being rejected so openly on an almost daily basis could not have been easy for the supporters to take.

With all these managers not wanting the job and with 'letters that would make you cry' from Steve Coppell there was so much mystery never solved regarding the City job. It was a job that no one seemed to want.

When Coppell walked out the City fans went ballistic. They needed some answers but weren't getting any information and of course in those situations, when there's a vacuum all sorts of rumours start off. It was silly season.

A number of players were getting the bird from the fans. Andy Dibble and Kit Symons were getting booed regularly. Those guys were both friends of mine and I also wanted to know what the fans were thinking and why they were booing.

There was an incident in a game against Lincoln City where there was an almighty cock-up between both of them which ended in a farcical goal for Lincoln. Sometimes, in football, these things happen and you want the ground to just swallow you up. In the eyes of the fans though, their view is that you simply weren't trying. Patience was running out.

Phil Neal came in for a short while. Rather than being remembered as the England and Liverpool captain who achieved so much as a player, he was thought of as the hapless 'Yes Boss' assistant to Graham Taylor in that memorable TV documentary *The Impossible Job*.

Frank Clark was eventually appointed as manager, technically our fifth in the last five months. He had done well recently with Nottingham Forest, finishing third in the Premier League and getting them into Europe. He had managed to handle the job of replacing Brian Clough and perhaps there was an idea around the club that he would be big enough to handle the hottest seat in football, the manager's chair at City.

A poisoned chalice they used to call it. Alan Ball, Asa Hartford, Steve Coppell, Phil Neal and now Frank Clark. Five managers in as many months. Cups for cock-ups.

The club had a share issue and further investment came into the club. More players were brought in under Clark. Soon afterwards, Bassett did turn up at Maine Road in the opposition dugout and got the bird from the City fans. At least Clark actually wanted the job and decided to take it.

To be fair to Clark the club only suffered one defeat in his first 12 games in charge so he did enjoy a brief honeymoon period of sorts and the fans were prepared to give him a chance. Still out of action, I had become a fan but was having to see the team in freefall.

Certain managers wouldn't want certain players. Bally was a bit like that but then with every new signing that came in there would just be more and more players joining the staff. I knew people on the inside but I felt completely on the outside. My main duty as a City player at that time was to hobble around on crutches saying 'hello' to any well-wishers.

While the club toiled on and off the pitch, I was falling further and further into a dark place. Lakey alluded to it in his excellent autobiography – depression – yet he managed to find the courage and strength to keep me going and perhaps at times I kept him going too.

When I started running again I found that I had a bit of gristle on my bone. It was on the joint line of my knee and it required a further operation to get things right. So that set me back again. It was a long struggle and at times I keep repeating myself but I didn't think I would ever get back from it.

Then all of a sudden you get the all-clear to step up training again and you keep everything crossed.

I couldn't take sitting there watching training let alone seeing some of the games. So me and Paul would meet at the Galleon Hotel in Didsbury. These were lonely times but these sessions were the only thing that seemed to be working – both physically and mentally. It got my knee strong but most of all it kept me sane. Lots of running, lots of weights and a 'safe' place to ask questions and get some of the answers I needed.

I would do anything to get my career back on track. As well as gym work, we kept our spirits up with constant banter and for him to take such an interest in me and my well-being after everything he'd been through speaks volumes for Paul as a man.

There are certain people I will always be grateful to. Dr Dandy of course for doing such a good job. Yes I've got two pins in my knee but it's been no trouble since I stopped playing. The other person I'll always have an enormous debt of gratitude to is Paul Lake, for the way he looked after me and gave me heartfelt advice and pointed me in the right direction.

Lakey was one of a number of people who spelt it out to me in no uncertain terms that I'd have to work doubly hard to get back to where I was and that's what we set out to do.

Paul had been through it all, he was a bit older than me and a bit wiser than me but he knew how to connect with me and get a grip on how I was feeling on any one given day. He'd done it himself, been there and got the t-shirt so I think that's the connection we had, he kind of took it upon himself to take me under his wing and ensure that it wasn't going to happen to me as well as him.

He had his own family and his own life going on but even with all that he took it upon himself to push me and push me and that's exactly what he did. Paul was a rock for me and was able to reassure me on days when I couldn't see any progress being made and he always had great advice on certain things because he could always speak from experience.

Up until this point the stuff that we were doing was only getting me so far. So Paul introduced me to Mandy and Phillipa, two physios who worked at the Beaumont Hospital in Bolton.

They had a hydrotherapy pool there and I'd undergo two sessions a week up at Bolton with two brilliant physios who just kept my spirits high.

Before I went to the Beaumont I would just run and run all day and eventually just hit the wall. However from here, I managed to make further progress.

Mandy and Phillipa would introduce hydrotherapy sessions and managed to take me to another level with swimming in the pool and strengthening exercises done in water with the water taking the weight.

You didn't have to force yourself to join in when Lakey was about doing his daft Eddie Murphy impressions first thing in the morning. Honestly, if he ever fancied it he would have probably make a brilliant stand-up comedian.

On some days, it wouldn't be about work, it might be a case of just going in and having a cup of tea with them. A chat. A friendly face. Someone to listen, someone to understand.

I remember doing a session on the grass outside the Beaumont. It was the first time I'd put my boots on to do some straight-line running and it was just an amazing feeling, to be stood outside in the fresh air with my football boots on and just being able to run again.

It was difficult to do that and then be told 'slow down now, that's enough', when I just wanted to push on and on as I could see some light at the end of the tunnel. The more progress the more motivation you have. I was getting closer to a comeback but I had to take care of myself.

By now we were into 1997 and the team had at last showed some fight and had given big-spending Middlesbrough a real game in the FA Cup. Ian Brightwell had a perfectly good goal disallowed.

Mathematically there was still a chance of the play-offs. That ended in March when former blue Fitzroy Simpson came back to score a late equaliser and stop the mini-run of wins which we were on. That particular night both City and United were at home, which doesn't normally happen in Manchester but on this occasion it did.

United were playing Porto in the Champions League and City were playing Portsmouth. United won at a canter and strode confidently on into the next round, whereas we were facing another season in what was then the First Division. The Blue fans would walk back into town as usual and have to take it on the chin from their sneering Red neighbours.

Fitzroy arrived at the club at a time when we were an established top-five team. So many players came and went through those doors during my time here it was just ridiculous. City fans will tell you that players we let go always had a habit of coming back and scoring against us. We had let so many go though it was bound to happen.

I would be looking at the table wondering what division I would be playing in the following year – if I came back. As a City player, you could be excused for asking that question quite a lot in those days.

Towards the end of that season I then went back to Platt Lane to continue my recovery. I was doing some straight-line running at Platt Lane in front of all the fans who used to come and watch at the back of the fence and in full view of the first-team squad who were all training.

I could run in a straight line but as soon as the cones came out to do some twisting and turning my knee would just swell up to the size of a balloon and I couldn't really understand it.

I would ice it and then the day after I would be fine again. The next day I'd resume training but again as soon as I'd do any diagonal running or change direction the problem would happen again.

They sent me for a scan and they found a piece of bone and gristle the size of a pea stuck in the joint line of my knee. I'd been out for almost 18 months by now and my knee had started swelling up again so it was back to wondering what I would do. The negative thoughts were coming back. Was I going to end up retiring?

I was quite down at this time. Nothing much anyone could say to me after being out for so long was going to change the way I felt and I started to think that everything was against me and it wasn't going to happen.

I'd seen the club relegated on the last game of the season against Liverpool and although we were now safe in the division following a few results under Frank Clark, I wanted to make the start of the following season and here was another setback.

In my later years I'd realised all these things had made me a stronger character to deal with a crowd booing me and come to terms with what I'd been through with my injury. Football can make you feel on top of the world or trapped and isolated.

I was sent for a small operation to clean out my knee a little bit, then it was another month of waiting before I could go back to running. I had done so many upper-body exercises that my physique had changed. It's true that I lost half a yard of pace after the injury but when I came back I was a lot more muscular.

The 1996/97 season was drawing to an end but eventually there seemed to be some light appearing at the end of the tunnel. The club had endured a topsy-turvy season but the general feeling was that the worst was over. With Clark a few months into the role there were signs of stability and perhaps a feeling that we could have a tilt at promotion the following season. I didn't know Clark that well but I was looking forward to working with him.

The last day saw a memorable game and incredible atmosphere against Reading where City were 2-0 down but bounced back to win 3-2. The stadium sang Georgi Kinkladze's name throughout and during the lap of honour he took an extra special bow. Certainly the fans were making it difficult for the club to sell him. In among all the mediocrity a flash of skill here and there from the little Georgian kept them going during those dark times.

The result showed at least there was a bit of fight coming back into the club and the crowd were as passionate as ever. Manchester City were a big club though and the expectation levels were always going to be sky high, as Clark was about to find out.

7

ARE YOU WATCHING MACCLESFIELD?

THERE was a buzz about the place in pre-season in 1997. We changed the club badge and we left Umbro, who had made City's kit since before the war. We now had the Kappa kit. A trendy kit manufacturer and with celebrity fans in Noel and Liam Gallagher there was still a quirkiness about Manchester City which appealed to the national media. The support stayed with the club again. We were – we still are – a unique club. City were still big news but not because of any fantastic results on the pitch.

Stephen Boler was still involved with the club. He had supported Peter Swales so many times before but he was too busy hunting white rhinos to attend the matches these days. He still provided a cash injection and some new players came in; Gerard Wiekens, Lee Bradbury, and Tony Vaughan to name just three. The fans were delighted that the little Georgian magician Kinkladze was still at the club. Uwe was still there too, in the final year of his contract. There was a feeling among the support that the season couldn't possibly be as bad as the previous campaign.

For me personally pre-season meant I was finally part of the first-team squad again. After a 21-month lay-off I was going back to work. Frank Clark had praised me in the media and welcomed me back into the fold. I wouldn't make the opening game of the season, he wouldn't rush me but I was involved in the pre-season build-up.

I remember a sunny evening in Blackpool where the City fans had obviously been on the lash most of the day and spent as much time on the pitch as off it. We were told they'd been running riot around the pleasure beach and lying down on the tram tracks pretending to be Alan Bradley out of *Coronation Street*!

It was great to be back involved with the guys and to be fair to Frank he was really supportive. Once I was close to first-team selection again he encouraged me a lot. That's the thing about being a footballer when you're injured. You don't feel you are of use to anyone. As I took part in pre-season training and continued my running and my strength work, more and more people would say, 'Morning, all right mate', and I would feel more a part of things again.

The opening day of the season brought the usual optimism, another full house and officially the start of the Kappa kit era. The colour of the kit had been tweaked to a laser blue colour instead of traditional sky blue and the traditional circular badge had been changed to a totally new design incorporating an eagle and three stars. This is City's current badge of course. It was changed because the club had sold the rights to the old badge and were losing money on merchandising sales. The kit had record sales so people must have liked it.

A 2-2 draw in the opening game against Portsmouth represented two dropped points. As it turned out those two dropped points on the opening day would come back to haunt us in a big way. Pompey would stay up on the last day of the season at our expense.

Then in midweek City lost at Blackpool in the League Cup and the second league game of that season saw a bad defeat at Sunderland in what was the opening fixture at their new Stadium of Light, including a goal from Niall Quinn against his old club.

It was not the flying start some had been predicting. Paper over the cracks and a lot of the same problems were there. Clark and Richard Money tried to instal discipline but there was no discipline under Clark. 'New kit, same shit' was one chant from the City supporters.

Early-season optimism had simply evaporated before I made my return. We had switched from a back four to a back three and then back again. We had taken two points from 12 in the league, an even worse start than under Alan Ball the previous season. We had looked nervous and short of pace as a side as we were dumped out of the League Cup by Blackpool on penalties in the second leg of that tie.

My own comeback was at Clark's former club Nottingham Forest. I remember being sat in the dressing room before the Forest game, reading texts from friends and family who knew I was going to be involved.

Knowing I was playing again was just a surreal moment. From lying in bed at the Bupa hospital 21 months ago to finally putting on my boots and going out to play to sitting there getting myself mentally prepared to face Pierre van Hooijdonk, Kevin Campbell and the rest of the Forest forward line. I was back in the saddle. I didn't have any great expectations for the game. The objective was to simply get through without the knee swelling up again. My mindset was, 'Tonight is important for the club but even more important for me, I've got to look after myself first.' It was probably selfish to just think of myself but that's how I felt.

It was probably our best result of the season. Forest had won their first four games and would eventually end up promoted but we played them off the park at the City Ground and beat them 3-1. The fans were in great voice behind the goal, shouting 'there's only one Frank Clark' for probably the last time ever. Forest would go on to win the championship with 94 points.

Sat back in the dressing room after that game I had the biggest, cheesiest grin on my face. I had done it! I'd got some good tackles in, some blood and thunder challenges. After 21 long months out, 21 months of self-doubt, loss of self-esteem, mental and physical pain and without a hiding place in the claustrophobic atmosphere of Manchester football I was back doing what I loved best. Playing for City.

A few people commented after the Forest game that I wasn't 'the same player any more' but I don't think I was ever going to be exactly the same player. I had to work harder in training to maintain my knee strength and initially my focus was simply about getting through as many games as I could.

Another objective was to avoid any niggly injuries. In all fairness I had lost half a yard of pace and I would go on to suffer from a series of daft knocks such as thigh strains, little imbalances which looking back I think hampered my career.

I was trying to cope with the difference in strength between my knees. My right knee was not as strong as the left one so my body would be over-compensating for that and that's basically where a lot of those annoying little injuries came from later on in my career.

We beat Swindon Town 6-0 on a warm autumn day. It looked as though on our day we could be a decent outfit. It was a strange league, anyone could beat anyone else and at that stage the table hadn't properly settled down yet. That was as good as it got though.

There was a weight of expectation on the squad that we should be right up there for promotion. The fans demanded success and rightly so. In their eyes they had shown loyalty, shelling out for season tickets again and showing patience with what was happening at the club. Money had been spent in the summer and the expectation around the club was promotion – however realistic or unrealistic that actually was.

The home form in particular turned out to be absolutely dreadful and a couple of bad defeats brought the return of a crisis of confidence among the playing staff, plus also the return of very angry demonstrations outside the main stand from fans who had come to the end of their tethers.

There was a group called Free The Manchester 30,000 who were calling for the head of Franny Lee. Franny had famously said he would jump off the top of the Kippax if City went down again. It was a tough time for the chairman, who by now was constantly under the spotlight from the media.

I played in a defeat at QPR when we wore that ridiculous yellow kit as a one-off and the travelling army sang 'we're gonna win the league' – but the sense of humour the City fans were known for was starting to run out. Supporters were calling the radio phone-ins to vent their anger at performances and at decisions made by Frank Clark. Two years out of football and I'd gone from one relegation battle in the Premier League straight into another one in a lower league.

My impression of Clark was that he didn't fit in with what was required at the club at that time. He obviously had a good track record. A great many managers had tried and failed when it came to City. Howard Kendall and Peter Reid did very well for the club. They were very tough and stuck by their decisions. I felt Clark was too soft at times. He just couldn't seem to stamp his authority on the place and the longer it would go on without him doing that, the more things deteriorated.

The club had a chairman who was known for being a strong character. The chairman prior to him, Peter Swales, was also known for being a strong character and while maybe not as hands-on as Franny he certainly cast a shadow over the manager's door. Clark had a decent start at City but then events just seemed to run away from him.

I was confident in my own ability but could see a general collective problem around the dressing room. A general lack of confidence about the place but Frank lacked the charisma, the personality, the whatever it was to lift the players. The times when he did go ballistic and try to get a reaction were memorable because they were rare.

If I made a mistake often I wouldn't even get a rollocking. Why not? Did he not even care?

He had Richard Money, the coach who worked with him, who was an extrovert and someone who always had something to say. Frank was totally different. He was very quiet and thoughtful. Maybe the way he carried himself put players off him.

Richard was very confident in himself and his own ability to get what he wanted out of the players and it would often be him and Alan Hill that would actually take training. I actually liked Alan. Out of the three of them, he was the one who seemed to talk the most sense. He had been a full-back in his playing career as well, which made certain points he wanted to make about the game easier to get across. Richard would do a lot of keep-ball sessions but other teams would just swarm us in that league and took the ball off us.

It must have been difficult for Frank at the time to come in and figure out what sort of team he was going to play. We used to go into Platt Lane some days and we'd have a corridor and there were dressing rooms there and every dressing room was full of players and the further you got down the corridor the closer you'd get to the actual 11 that were playing at that time.

As you went down the corridor you could pick out people like Nigel Clough and Gerry Creaney, players on big wages who weren't even getting on the bench… we had a lot of different players who the fans weren't even seeing and the club were paying them fortunes. Sometimes they would have to get the odd game to put them in the shop window.

Eddie McGoldrick had come in and the fans liked his all-action style. Dalian Atkinson had been in on loan and we had the other Georgians on the books, Murtaz Sheila, Kakhabar Tchdadzse and Mikhail Kavelashvili.

We had a lot of players who thought they should be playing every week, regardless of who had the shirt at that time. Some players used to laugh and joke about Clark. He had a guitar in his office and they used to knock on his door then go in and he'd be sat up in the office playing the guitar with his feet up on the desk!

This was alluded to by someone on *Fantasy Football League* with David Baddiel and Frank Skinner, which was a popular TV show at the time. It was the start of fans picking their dream teams or fantasy league teams and there was a feature on Clark sitting on the bus at Forest belting out all these daft songs.

The fans at first liked what they saw in Clark, shouting 'Frankie Clark's blue and white army' but as the winter of discontent developed the mood changed significantly throughout the club and among the fanbase.

We had over 50 players at the club and some of them we just couldn't move on. Some of them rarely played and some played just a handful of games. I've mentioned the players who would be knocking on the manager's door demanding to play. Others would be quite happy to sit back and just collect their wages.

With all the managers I'd worked with at that stage I'd never really had that sort of attitude where if I wasn't playing I'd go banging on the door. It had never happened before – if something was wrong I'd just get on with my job. We had a lot of those sorts of players at the time but then again I was younger and I was being picked more often than not so I had less of an axe to grind with the manager.

One night that autumn news came through of a serious crash on the M56 motorway. Nicky Summerbee and Gio Kinkladze had been speeding irresponsibly and some City fans had been racing down to the scene as soon as the news broke – to take pieces of Georgi's Ferrari away as mementos would you believe!

Just when you think it couldn't get any worse at this club it always does. Gio had 38 stitches but he was back the very next week. The pair were the subjects of countless wind-ups over the next few weeks. We never let them forget about it.

Another trip to Chester races – maybe we went there more than I first thought – and we were in the VIP enclosure. Jeff Whitley had been spotted by a City fan.

'Are you Jeff Whitley?'

'Yes love.'

'Can I have a picture on my phone with you?'

'Yes of course love.'

Ten minutes later, up she comes again. 'Jeff, will you speak to my boyfriend, he's a big City fan too,' so he speaks to the boyfriend. A few minutes later, 'Jeff, will you speak to my mum…Jeff will you speak to my mate,' and on it went.

This fan was getting on Jeff's nerves and then there was one request too many. 'Jeff, will you speak to my…' and before she could finish the sentence Jeff grabbed the phone and sent it flying 30 yards away. Jeff was pushed to the limit but he had his problems back then and the drink would change his personality.

Him and Michael Brown lived together in Cheadle for a while which was probably the worst thing that could have happened to both of them. They would egg each other on and have mad parties. We'd often have the police turn up at the training ground the following Monday asking questions or fishing for information.

Jeff especially was trying to burn the candle at both ends in those days. He would turn up drunk at training but still put in a great shift. He would still be at the front of the group for running and would put 100 per cent in every day. He was the type of guy who trained hard but played hard too.

Ten years to the day since the club beat Huddersfield Town 10-1 in a famous win, we lost 1-0 at home to the same opposition. It was a landmark game in the season. It was the game where the fans realised we could actually go down again.

Huddersfield were bottom of the table and we were all over them for 75 minutes but just couldn't put our chances away. The fans stayed with us while it was 0-0 and they were very vocal in their backing for City, especially in the North Stand.

As soon as Huddersfield scored with 15 minutes to go the crowd turned on the whole team with 'you're not fit to wear the shirt', 'we're shit and we're sick of it' ,'sack the board' and a host of other chants.

Up until that point, individuals such as Nicky Summerbee and Kit Symons had been the prime targets for the boo boys

– in fact Kit had started that season as club captain and had been booed throughout the season – but on this occasion the vitriol was not aimed at one particular player, it was the whole team.

The rising sense of frustration exploded that night. There was nowhere to hide and there were riots outside the ground for an hour. The fans had just had enough. They were questioning the players' attitude, questioning the players' pride and the general direction of the club.

It's always gone on at City. Look at the stick guys like Aleksandar Kolarov, Samir Nasri, Martin Demichelis and Edin Dzeko have got at times at home games in recent years. It's a different kind of pressure these days. The crowd are expecting wins all the time and if it's only 0-0 or things aren't going to plan there's always a scapegoat and they'll soon get on a player's back during the game.

As a group we felt under real pressure at Maine Road because of the expectation levels and for some of the playing staff the size of the crowds undoubtedly added even more mental pressure on to them.

By now speculation about the chairman was ongoing in the media. The players couldn't lift it, the management couldn't lift it. We were in freefall again.

What was happening at the club at that time was farcical. It is amazing to think how bad the spiral of decline had become. People often said in the media some of the managers the club had in those days never realised how big the job was. The expectation levels were always there even though we'd been dwindling along, changing manager after manager, bringing in player after player and not really seeing any improvement on the pitch. It was said the Peter Swales era lacked stability but it was a similar scenario during this particular time too.

We were not really producing any good football at this time and much was made of the amounts of money being paid for, and being paid to, certain players. Lee Bradbury came in for some fierce criticism and picked up the nickname 'Lee Badbuy'.

I would go out and about in Manchester at that time and have conversations with supporters in the streets. My abiding memory was that the fans genuinely felt this group of players didn't care about what was happening to the club and you know what, perhaps some of them didn't. We had a core of players though, the main ones who would try and get things going but we would have to carry others who were there to simply pick up their wages.

This season, together with the following season, were the darkest times to be a City player, a City director, a City fan. At that time the club were viewed as a joke. As a player you couldn't turn off the telly, you couldn't avoid the papers, the situation was there every day. There was no hiding place for fans or players in those days. You simply couldn't get away from it.

The public might think of Frank Clark as being generally quite calm but after some games he did lose the plot. Things were beginning to take their toll on him. I'm not sure how much pressure he was getting from upstairs but as time went on his powers seemed to wane.

Kevin Horlock was someone who always gave 100 per cent to the cause but even he was singled out after one particularly bad result at Maine Road. It was a windy and rainy night. Frank came in the dressing room after a truly abysmal team display and went round each player one by one having a right go about every single aspect of their performance.

Suddenly he turned round to Kev and just let rip at him. One minute he was talking about the game, next minute screaming 'and you, in your fucking Porsche' at the top of his voice.

It all just seemed strange, a few of the lads couldn't believe what they were hearing.

Kev had told us beforehand though how he was sat at a crossroads on his way into the game and the manager had driven past nearly straining his neck in order to see who it was in this new Porsche.

Kev had moved down in his seat with his flat cap on but Frank had seen him and given him an absolute rollocking after the game. I think it was mentioned in one of his press conferences afterwards about players, the cars they drove and perhaps they should be trying to give a bit more effort.

I remember before the injury playing under Alan Ball and the feeling among certain players that they just didn't want to come in to work for him. Here I was again having fought for my career and it was even worse. Players were going missing, there was no spark at all, and having been out so long I just wanted to get back involved but had I not been injured I might have been more inclined to knock on a manager's door and ask how things had got so bad.

But I just didn't feel I had the authority to do that. I didn't particularly want to play in a bad team where other people weren't pulling their weight. Managers had come and gone and so if there were problems nobody knew who to go and speak to. Staff nights out weren't taking place. Cliques had developed. It was awful.

The England players of that particular time always laugh about Eileen Drewery with her warm hands and the time when she was brought in by Glenn Hoddle – 'put your hands in my hands boys and tell me all your problems!'

We had a bizarre one too at City that season. Richard Money was lively around the lads and was always one to join in with the group, befriending them and coming up with nicknames for players, and naturally we all thought he was joking when one day he said Clark was bringing a fitness trainer in with him who he had used at Forest and he was the spitting image of Wayne Sleep.

As you can imagine the lads used to rip into him on a daily basis – he tried to get us to do different things that they had worked on before at Forest and they seemed to think that would work quite well. They didn't. Arsene Wenger getting rid of Jaffa Cakes and Jelly Babies from the coach journeys is one thing. Getting footballers to re-enact The Nutcracker is another.

He had us doing some silly things at times and the lads used to slaughter him. Eventually there was a bit of conflict there because some of the lads didn't quite understand why they were being asked to do the things they were doing. In the end it just added to the general feeling of farce around the club. No one knew what on earth was going to happen next. Give me cross-country running in the mud around Wythenshawe Park with Skip over that any day of the week.

Rumours were rife that the manager was going to be sacked, but the chairman wouldn't cancel his holiday to call an extraordinary general meeting with the rest of his board and no change took place. At Barnsley the fans sang 'I'd rather be in Barnsley than Barbados!' which went down like a lead balloon with Franny. Yet every now and again we'd get the odd mad result, for instance beating promotion-challenging Middlesbrough 2-0. That was the one time I can remember us getting one over on Middlesbrough in my time at the club.

Those days where we played with freedom and really expressed ourselves were few and far between though. Most of the time we played with fear. We owed Middlesbrough from the year before in the cup and maybe as the opposition were the fancied club for once that worked in our favour.

The Lincoln manager John Beck had said earlier that season that as a club we might have to drop down again to sort out some of the problems we had and Franny Lee had gone mental when he heard that comment. It kind of hung in the air though. Someone had dared to say that we could drop down yet another division which would be unthinkable for a club of Manchester City's stature.

As the season went on that fear was always prominent. A lack of confidence swept through the place. Rumour had it that Joe Royle was offered the Northern Ireland job but turned it down because he was waiting for the call from City. It didn't come until mid-February, six weeks later. When you think we went down on the last day on goal difference, changing the manager earlier might have done the trick. Royle had supposedly turned down 14 different positions in the months leading up to finally taking over at Maine Road.

Things came to a head after the Valentine's Day game with Bury at Maine Road, a famous game and a famous win for the Shakers. It may have been Valentine's Day but there was very little in the way of love in the air around the place and on that day the fans demonstrated inside the ground against the players, against the manager and against the chairman.

The City fans actually applauded the Bury players off the pitch. The calls for both Clark and Lee to go during the game were loud and repetitive and as players we were just aware that it was very restless all around. After the game there was yet another demonstration outside the ground. Maine Road was a very unhappy place. One supporter ran on to the pitch and ripped up his season ticket in the centre circle. Apparently someone at the club stuck it back together again and posted it back to him saying we all feel the same but you are not allowed to walk out on the club. We have to keep going and so should you!

Clark found out about his sacking in true City style – in the car park at Platt Lane. In came Joe Royle and for me personally this was the best thing that could have happened to me at the time.

My contract was running out but Joe made it clear I was part of his plans and he wanted me to be part of things. That was good enough for me. I signed another four-year deal at a time when I didn't know which league I would be playing in the following season.

The fans always used to talk about this supposed 'fifth column' around the club. Was I ever aware of players having relations with the media? Feeding stories to Paul Hince or Bryan Brett in the press if they weren't getting a game? I can honestly say, from my personal experience, that players weren't the source of leaks. One or two might have had good relations with the press but not many, not like now. Things did get into the press but half the time it was utter cobblers.

One of the nationals printed a story that I had turned a new contract down at a time when I was already on, wait for it, £17,500 a week! I wish! What a load of old bollocks. I rang them up. I'm not having people thinking I'm on nearly 20 grand a week and turning deals down because it's not enough money. 'Who's giving you this information?' I said. 'We are not allowed to say. It's confidential.' 'Well it's rubbish anyway, can you print an apology?'

Nowadays I have my own Twitter account but back then if I'd have had Twitter I could have just put out a statement and cleared it up immediately. Who knows whether it was just made up or whether it was a plant by someone at the club trying to make life hard for me?

I remember the first day's training we did with Joe. Everything was based around regaining confidence and putting a smile back on your face. Joe breezed in with a great air of confidence and an assured manner. He had good staff around him. In the first training session he spoke to the group straight away and you could see everyone's shoulders raise a few inches, he brought that confidence back to the lads. He cracked a few jokes. He tried to stop the pressure transmitting itself to the players.

He had a smile on his face and a relaxed but determined manner about him – businesslike – and he managed to convey that air of confidence over to the group.

Joe's job was a difficult one. Coming in as a former City player and with having other former players on his staff perhaps some people thought he would get instant results but the underlying problems at the club were deep-rooted by then. I maintain if he'd have come in a little bit earlier he'd have probably saved us from being relegated.

He tried to instil a common purpose around the club that everyone should want the same thing for the club. The fans were relieved that someone who understood the club's DNA was finally in charge.

Success. How could he achieve that with 50-odd players and many of them just there for the money with no chance of getting a game?

Before Joe came in, work wasn't a nice place to be. The staff that came in lifted things a little. Under Clark we had a fitness coach, Peter Edwards, but the players would be unfit. Willie Donachie came in, the training regime changed and the mentality changed.

Looking back we just ran out of time.

Joe inherited a ridiculous number of players and probably had to decide early on which ones he would be going with in the main. Maybe two or three others would be given a chance but overall it would be the ones who were showing they wanted to roll their sleeves up and work.

Sometimes in training the players who were just there for the money would be the victims of the odd tough challenge. Some of the coaching staff felt there was nothing wrong with that. Let them give a response back and show some passion.

Willie introduced discipline and had the players eating together after training to develop a bit of togetherness. Before that the lads would eat what they wanted after training. They would head off to the Rolling Pin sandwich shop or one of the many Caribbean restaurants in the vicinity of Maine Road. The first-team squad would eat together and even the club staff would be present although they would be sat on separate tables. It was about building a spirit in the club that was lacking previously. The diet was healthier – chicken, fish, pasta and salads were on the menu.

Joe took to his job with confidence and to be fair to the squad there was a response from the players. Although ultimately we would end up finishing in the bottom three Joe would eventually go on to transform a club that was beset by problems, or 'Cityitis' as he famously described it.

Other managers tried and failed miserably to sort out the problems at the club. Having 54 pros at a club would take its toll on any new manager but Joe handled it really well. He knew who and what he wanted from his team. First and foremost he just wanted players whose hearts were in it and who were prepared to work hard for each other. One of those signings that I remember who fitted into that category was Shaun Goater.

I'd previously played against Shaun in a reserve game when he was at Rotherham. I played at centre-half against him that night and I remember him elbowing me and jumping into me constantly! He certainly knew how to put himself about.

He had arrived at the club after we'd had all of the high-profile big-money signings such as Lee Bradbury and when we signed him, at the time I remember thinking, 'Well I know him but hang on, we're only paying £400,000 for someone who is not particularly well known – is this the guy to really lead the line for Manchester City and get us up the table?'

When he came in he had a special presence about him. Breezing into training with a big smile on his face, he got to know everyone really well immediately. He worked his socks off in training and just seemed to start to score goals straight away. It would go in off his shin pad, his knee, his nipple even (ask Wigan about that!). A striker has to get into those positions though in order to score those goals however scrappythey are, so that highlighted his outstanding work-rate.

We just knew on a matchday that we'd get something from him and he was a great lad too. There was great banter with him. Always smiling, always happy – happy to offer a bit of advice too, if you were down and out, if you'd had a bad game, he'd lift you up with his smile and infectious character.

For me he was one of the main signings Joe made. Shaun ended up proving a lot of people wrong, including some supporters who had told him face-to-face at meetings in the early part of his career that they felt he wasn't good enough in their eyes to put on that blue shirt. Shaun simply turned that criticism into a source of motivation.

Previously you'd be sat in the dressing room and certain players would stand up ranting and raving in front of managers, all for show. Asking for commitment but then ducking out of the first challenge, the first tackle. Joe and Willie could see through people like that.

The dressing room regained a common purpose. Having a hierarchy of former players is not a bad thing. Players tend to listen to people who have a presence about them, and very rarely would they dare to take the piss out of them.

Willie Donachie and Asa Hartford. Tough Scots who had the club in their hearts. They tried to instil a bit of fight among the place. Alex Stepney the goalkeeping coach. Roy Bailey, Ronnie Evans, even Dr Luft who occasionally came on away trips with us. I felt we had a good staff around us who kept everything ticking along.

With Joe and Willie at first you might think they were chalk and cheese. Willie didn't say a lot but when he did you listened. Willie led by example. He could outrun anyone in training. He was as fit as a fiddle.

Willie was acutely aware that confidence was down among the players and he would come up with loads of different ideas to try and keep things fresh. He was very big on the psychology of it all, anything to give the players some kind of competitive advantage.

I mentioned he instigated getting everyone to eat together. He also changed the routine around home games. He was big on us getting together beforehand and arriving together. Under Peter Reid we did something similar for a while, meeting together at the Copthorne Hotel and eating as a group and staying together the night before. Under Alan Ball players turned up for home games individually, and certainly after training couldn't wait to get away from the place.

We would vary where we'd train to get away from the media spotlight. Often we went to the Brooklands Sports Club in Sale. Before games we'd go over to St Francis's School, in the shadow of the Kippax, and have a kickabout in the playground there. Willie loved the club and I think he wanted the players to see the fans making their way to the ground and make that connection in their minds that the club belonged to the fans.

With two of my brothers.

The day I was spotted by City playing for Slumberland Rangers.

Horton hails Edghill debut

THE KID'S A KNOCKOUT

By Paul Hince

BRIAN HORTON today hailed last night's debut by teenager Richard Edghill as "the best I've seen from a kid his age."

Manchester City's Liverpool-born defender – still three days away from his 18th birthday – was drafted in for his senior bow against Wimbledon at Selhurst Park at the last moment, when Terry Phelan was ruled out with an Achilles injury.

And, against the toughest opponents in English soccer, the youngster responded with a show which even had the Wimbledon fans applauding.

"I don't think I've seen a debut as good as that from a boy of Richard's age," said Blues boss Horton.

"He is quick and incredibly assured when in possession for someone without any previous senior experience.

Comforting

"He took my eye in a practice game the other week, and I have excellent reports about his display in our friendly in Turkey last Tuesday.

"He did himself and his club proud, and, as a new manager, it is comforting for me to know that we have players of his quality coming through."

Manager Horton was also delighted with his other debutant, £1.6m defender Alan Kernaghan.

"Alan did everything I expected of him," adds Horton. "To say that Wimbledon are a handful up front is an understatement but Alan gave as good as he took."

Less pleasing for the Maine Road boss is the increasing list of injuries.

Latest casualties are David White (ankle), Terry Phelan (Achilles) and Rick Holden (ankle). They have only an outside chance of being fit for tomorrow night's Coca-Cola Cup-tie against Reading at Maine Road.

■ YOU NEED HANS . . . Wimbledon 'keeper Hans Segers punches clears as City striker Niall Quinn goes up for a header at Selhurst Park last night

Ranson's cup fight

RAY RANSON is fighting for fitness in an attempt to face the Manchester City side he was a member of only four months ago.

The veteran fullback has missed the last two games for his new club, Reading, but has set his heart of making a return to Maine Road for tomorrow's Coca-Cola Cup-tie.

"I was looking forward particularly to marking Rick Holden but I know he has been having injury problems, too," said Ranson, who still lives in Cheshire and trains with City.

My debut at Wimbledon.

On England under-21 duty.

Ryan Giggs – a tricky opponent to say the least!

We've done it!

Wembley 99 – and wearing a daft blue wig!

With the Goat – what a contribution he made.

Getting stuck in with another tackle.

Celebrating my goal against Blackburn.

In battle against West Brom on a day I was sent off.

Celebrating at Blackburn in that famous win.

Shielding the ball from former City player Ashley Ward.

In competition with Blackburn's Damien Duff.

Keep Right On – a loan period at Birmingham City.

Cover star of the QPR programme when they played City in the League Cup.

Wedding celebrations with Eve.

Cassie and Olivia, my great kids.

My superb girls.

Family fun.

It's mine! With my hands on the Premiership trophy.

They had worked all week to come and see you play and so that way the players knew what it meant to people to be a player for Manchester City.

We'd get warmed up and the fans would see us arrive in a minibus at 2.45pm and we'd then walk straight into the stadium when it was really busy outside. This was all designed so that we would feel the warmth and the love from the crowd and it was all intended to take the fear away or reduce the fear levels around; to have that visual impact on seeing our fans close up and knowing there were behind you, on your side and to get us all used to the noise levels and the expectation all around us.

Crowds of 30,000-plus can be all well and good when things are going great but they can be a tough audience if the team aren't up to the job in hand. Sometimes these psychology tactics would work, sometimes they didn't but at least the management had been brave enough to think outside the box and had tried to shake things up. They looked at anything which would make playing at Maine Road a real 'home advantage'. If it didn't work we'd scrap it and try something new.

Stockport County at home was an emphatic win but it didn't mean we were out of the woods. We had a point to prove following the terrible 3-1 defeat at Edgeley Park earlier in the season and this game saw the return of Ian Bishop. Eddie McGoldrick was in the opposition team. It was the one time we were out of the bottom three after that game.

We'd had a bad game at home to Oxford United beforehand. They were one of a number of clubs around us in the table who brought their A-game to Maine Road and just bullied us off the pitch. One of their players even started on Willie Donachie in the technical area and Willie did very well to restrain himself.

Another was Birmingham City at home. A late, late winner for them from Dele Adebola when he should not have still been on the pitch after clashing with Richard Jobson was difficult to take. We were deep into stoppage time and had to finish the game with ten men only for Adebola himself, unpunished by the referee, to bag his winner.

In certain games we played awfully while in others we just didn't have the luck, hitting the bar and the ball bouncing out instead of creeping over the line. Missing sitters from four yards out. We did everything but score in this game.

Away to Wolverhampton Wanderers we were on course for a win but a fumble from Martyn Margetson meant two points dropped in a 2-2 draw. So many points were dropped and we were unable to get a run together which would have put pressure on the sides around us. It was a case of little things going against you, terrible individual mistakes, not being able to hold on to leads when you had them.

QPR was the last home game of the season and it was must-win. I remember being in the tunnel and Vinny Jones was going round the corridors shouting his mouth off, asking where this 'Kinkladze fella' was. Gio had been out of the side for a few weeks but Joe brought him back for this game. It was a move which certainly made the City fans excited.

QPR were still in trouble near the foot of the table. Lining up in the tunnel Jones tried to intimidate Kinkladze, grabbing him roughly by the throat and trying to shake him up a bit.

Georgi went out on to the pitch and gave the perfect response by curling home an absolute screamer of a free kick after about 90 seconds and then he ran off waving at Vinny, saying something to him as he went past him.

Gio could create something out of nothing but also if he didn't get the protection he needed he couldn't produce what he wanted to produce. At times it looked like he was exactly what we needed but overall we struggled that season. The odd good result. The odd glimpse of genius. Joe felt he was a luxury player and the situation he inherited meant in his eyes we couldn't afford to carry any luxury players.

This was the infamous game where Jamie Pollock headed that ridiculous own goal past Martyn Margetson. The Pollock goal is just incredible. It's one of the most popular clips on YouTube, especially with fans of Queens Park Rangers. It's a little bit like Gazza's goal against Scotland at Euro 96 but in a gone-wrong type of fashion.

Pollock scooped the ball up after running on to meet his own touch then leapt up to lob the keeper but all while facing the wrong way. Given the context of the game and the importance of the result that day it was a crushing, devastating moment. QPR fans later voted Jamie Pollock as the most important person ever in history – even more important than Jesus Christ.

That day the club had paid for a banner which all the players had to carry out as a thank-you to the fans. It said, 'City…the best team in the land…in all the world.' The famous chant is actually, 'City…the best team in the land…AND all the world.' Even a simple thing like that they couldn't get right.

A 2-2 draw meant it was out of our hands going to Stoke the following weekend.

The Stoke game. An incredible build-up in the week but horrible knowing it might still be out of our hands even if we won. The City fans will tell you that feeling of absolute dread of another possible relegation on the last day of the season. They were experienced in this emotion, hardened by it even.

They had been there so many times before – 1983, 1987 and 1996 were all settled on the last day – and the only saving grace was that Portsmouth and Port Vale, our main relegation rivals, were both away from home that day too.

The City fans were buying tickets in the home end in the lead-up to the game and as well as the 5,000 behind the goal there were estimates of another 4,000 in with the Stoke fans. One thing we did know was that we would be well supported at Stoke.

A minute or so into the game, it became apparent in the stadium who supported who and it was going off in all the stands around us and fans spilled on to the pitch. The game carried on although it must have been a close call in terms of taking the players off.

In those circumstances you just play on and wait for any instructions from the referee.

The atmosphere was tense and electric and a mixture of very hot weather and a lot of alcohol being consumed by the fans meant anything was liable to happen in the stands. You could feel it and maybe it got to the Stoke players more than it did to us.

On the day we actually put in a fantastic performance, one our fans could be proud of. We went down fighting but it was too little too late.

Gio had been playing for Georgia the day before but Joe wanted him to play again within 24 hours so he had only arrived back in Manchester at 2am. He had a bit of jet lag but had a decent game.

Shaun Goater put us into a 1-0 lead at half-time and Paul Dickov doubled that after the break. Stoke then pulled one back but within a minute Lee Bradbury headed us 3-1 ahead which killed the game and all but sent Stoke down.

When Shaun went through to make it 4-1, at the actual moment of that goal there was still hope. Port Vale were two goals to the good at Huddersfield but Portsmouth were only one up away at Bradford City. Port Vale had scored in the very first minute so the fans were keeping their fingers crossed hoping that Portsmouth might just slip up.

It is amazing to think of it when you see what a major force Manchester City are now that the fans on that day were glued to their radios listening out for scores from their relegation rivals, Port Vale and Portsmouth. It beggars belief.

Shaun made it 4-1 and we looked over to the bench. There were no smiles, no clenched fists, no thumbs-up gestures. In fact the news had got much worse. As we were celebrating both Portsmouth and Port Vale had scored again. The players knew it. The fans knew it. Everyone knew it. We were down.

The City fans then thundered out their heartfelt love for the club, 'Man City, Man City, We'll support you evermore', 'I know I am, I'm sure I am, I'm City 'til I die' and unbelievably with our derbies now seemingly against a team from Cheshire that used to be in the Conference, 'Are you watching Macclesfield?' The gallows humour stayed with the supporters until the very end.

The game petered out and it felt like a testimonial at the end. Kevin Horlock grabbed our fifth and final goal and then the referee put everyone out of their misery. It was shattering and for the first few minutes as it sank in, the dressing room was a desperate place.

Before that fateful afternoon at Leeds I was perhaps on the verge of an England call-up and now I was back to full fitness yet I was going to be a Third Division player. That's football.

I was going to stay at the club regardless but knew some others would have to be paid off. Uwe was going, Kinky was going and there would have to be a major clear-out. A lot of players were on big money though so it wouldn't be straightforward at all to simply move players on.

The push for promotion started the second the final whistle went at Stoke. Joe got us in the changing rooms and laid it out to us for everyone to understand that the next season, pre-season would be a gruelling affair and that we'd be fit and ready for the start of the competitive fixtures. I was personally encouraged by a lot of what Joe said after that game and with the pressure of the relegation battle over surely we could consolidate and come back.

Relegation to the third tier was the culmination of years of mistakes. Changing managers, buying player after player, spending ridiculous amounts of money. The decline had started under Peter Swales. Franny Lee couldn't turn things around and left before the second relegation was confirmed. New chairman David Bernstein wrote to all the supporters to apologise on behalf of the club and to ask them for their support once again next season.

There was a famous image of a young City fan in tears at Stoke, Leighton Gobbett, wiping his eyes with a flag. Bernstein framed that picture, framed it and put it on his desk. He used that as motivation to drive the club back to where they should be. Everyone at the club had a duty, a part to play to ensure we would come back.

It must have felt like the end for some fans though that afternoon, especially as they went back up the M6 to Manchester with no windows on their coaches after major trouble outside at the end.

As a player you go on holiday but it was a horrible feeling all summer. You are there thinking, 'Surely this has to be rock bottom now, surely things couldn't get any worse. Could they?'

8

THIS IS HOW IT FEELS TO BE CITY

THE summer of 1998 was a terrible time for all connected with Manchester City. We were sat in the Second Division and being laughed at by everyone. There were a few jokes doing the rounds at this time that our fans had to put up with.

One involved Franny Lee going shopping at Kendals and getting in the lift. He sees an old lady struggling with a few bags. Quick as a flash, Franny leans over to help her. 'Can you manage, love?' he says. She replies, 'No Franny I don't want your stupid job either.'

Next was Franny Lee in a hotel getting in a lift and ending up on the wrong floor where a conference is taking place. 'Where am I ?' says Franny. 'You're in the conference sir,' says the lift concierge. 'The conference?' squeals Franny. 'But what happened to divisions one and two?'

Other jokes involved a play on words. What does CITY stand for? Conference In Two Years. There was another one later when EIDOS became our shirt sponsors…Every Idiot

Dreaming of Success. Later it was changed to Eleven Idiots Dreaming of Success. You get the drift.

I knew plenty of fans and they were going through it. People try to make out there are gloryhunters in our support now but the people who went to City in those days will tell you how hard things were. Plenty of those same fans will have gone to Barcelona, Madrid, Dortmund and Munich in recent seasons and enjoyed their nights out.

Pre-season came round so quickly that summer. I think they wanted us in earlier than normal for the sake of our fitness and for the sake of our minds because they knew we'd be dwelling on things over the summer.

The wounds were open for the players. We'd played poorly and to go into that situation at Stoke where we won yet everyone else around us also won was frustrating beyond belief. You look back at all the points dropped, all the missed opportunities, the manner in which we threw some of those games away. It wasn't anything to be particularly proud of.

Joe had given a rousing speech at the end of the Stoke game and left everyone in no uncertain terms as to what was expected moving forwards.

I managed to stay injury-free in this season. I would need all of my powers to fight, scrap and battle my way to the finishing line come May. Getting a full pre-season under my belt was imperative.

It was a collective failure that had led the club to this position but even though I cared very much for the club I still didn't see myself as the kind of person who would automatically feel they should be going round to other people and lecturing them on what they should or shouldn't be doing. Certainly there were some frustrating characters in the dressing room. People who lacked heart, who lacked commitment. I felt and I was sure from speaking to our supporters that I wasn't someone who fitted into those categories.

Joe had brought in Richard Jobson, who he used to work with at Oldham, and he would act as a calming influence on some of the younger players within that dressing room. I noted that I classed myself as being one of the younger players taking advice from Jobbo! Richard had been on the Leeds side the day I suffered my horrendous injury at Elland Road.

He was a nice guy coming to the end of his career but he had captain qualities. Both himself and Andy Morrison for example were natural leaders but we would all go about our tasks in different ways. Andy would be more vocal than Richard or myself but we would all be able to get our points across when necessary.

Jobbo was a prime example of what a good and long career you could have if you looked after yourself. Jobbo always gave you confidence if you were playing alongside him and he would be continually talking to you throughout the game.

With the injury it was more apparent that I had lost just a touch of pace, perhaps half a yard, but looking at someone like Jobbo, who read the game so well and timed his interceptions to perfection, I could use him as an example of someone who continued to make a difference even in the autumn of his career. He showed the importance of staying mentally strong and focused and not to be too concerned about the pace side of the game.

During that close-season people didn't actually know at first how the City fans would respond. Would they keep going each week? Would they stay with us after so many relegations, so many yo-yo years and so many broken promises? Franny Lee had resigned after the Port Vale game back in March. The new chairman, David Bernstein, wrote to all season ticket holders to apologise for the mistakes of the past and to plead for their support again this season. Some 14,000 bought season tickets.

Joe Royle was someone the City supporters trusted and there was no way they would let the club die. They could envisage an upturn. Playing for City no matter what league we were in always felt like playing for a big club, an important club with a history.

If we thought dropping down again would mean the club falling off the radar and no one taking an interest in our fortunes we couldn't have been more wrong. More and more over the summer it sank in where we were. Yet the club still had a masterplan and needed to gain a couple of quick promotions from here to make it work.

They had done a deal with Sport England and Manchester City Council and the club were going to be taking over the running of the new Commonwealth Games stadium after the event in 2002. City were the only viable tenants in the area.

We had the support base already there and the way that Maine Road had been rebuilt in the all-seater era – with different shades of blue seats and with the 'Gene Kelly' stand, the uncovered bit in the corner which didn't actually even face the pitch – well, the new stadium would put an end to all that and be a new start for the club. The fans called it the 'Gene Kelly' because it was uncovered, it was the 'singing in the rain' stand in their eyes!

Chris Bird was also on board by now and one of his jobs was to stem the negative tide of PR the club were experiencing. The press were wiping the floor with the club but he came in and added a touch of professionalism. I liked Chris, I got on well with him. I had time for him and he had time for me. One of his other roles was to work on the project for the new stadium.

Back-to-back promotions would offer a degree of success and would wake up the fanbase so that the new ground would be filled. There was some criticism early on that the stadium wasn't going to be used as an athletics arena after the Games but people forget the Commonwealth Games only took place in Manchester because the stadium was guaranteed an 'anchor tenant' in the form of Manchester City, so there was never going to be a situation like the one in Sheffield where the Don Valley Stadium became a white elephant the city's taxpayers couldn't afford.

A glorious new stadium seemed a world away at the start of the 1998/99 campaign. Joe had been tearing his hair out over some of the drinking at the club which was still continuing.

We were all assembling for the pre-season photograph on the pitch at Maine Road and the manager seemed to be running late but all the players were there waiting for him. Eventually Joe came down the tunnel and shouted straight across to Jeff Whitley and Michael Brown, 'You two…off the photograph! So you can learn to stay in and stop drinking you are not going on the photograph!' They were eventually allowed on the photo.

Jeff's problems have been well documented but in those days some of the boys would always be out drinking, always pulling girls and through horseplay and hi-jinks more than anything else getting into trouble from time to time. It had started to have an effect on everyone else in the dressing room though. He won't mind me saying this but Jeff was like a dog with two dicks in those days!

We had a tough pre-season, training with the Royal Navy down at HMS Torpoint in Devon. The games were going to come thick and fast and it would be a long old season.

One of the proudest moments in my City career was when I walked out with the team on the first day of that season, against

Blackpool. A full house and the stadium was packed with colour, noise, passion and hope. These fans didn't desert the club in their hour of need. I remember the feeling walking off at Stoke and how low I felt and then this, the very next league game and even though we were even lower down the league structure it somehow felt better. It felt like a new start, like a weight lifted from our shoulders, and we could try again.

It was a memorable sight and a good solid start to the season. We soon found out though that it was to be a very unforgiving league with every club in that division treating us as their cup final and playing 20 per cent better than they normally do in other league games. We were warned about this but we didn't know what was happening to us and couldn't get to grips with the intensity and desire from the other teams. It was literally half a season before we were able to start imposing ourselves on to teams in that division.

The following week we had Fulham away. They had in their side Peter Beardsley, who had been with us the season previously for a while. Mohammed Al Fayed had brought in Kevin Keegan and here was a club that was arguably better-placed for going up than we were. They brought us back down to earth with a thumping 3-0 defeat.

The first half of that season was a total nightmare. I was already City's longest-serving player by now having only been in the first team for five seasons. When you think of how many players had been on our books throughout my time that just shows the stability or rather the lack of it that was around the place at the time. I felt my own form was good. I was fit and contributing and in terms of my own career, having been out for so long I was happy to get games under my belt.

A lot of people have commented on the arrival of Andy Morrison and pointed out that it was one of our turning points, along with Terry Cooke and the Goater–Dickov partnership starting to gel. There's no doubt Andy made an impact. He was introduced to the team in the dressing room and then he was off again for about three days, I think he had one or two personal problems to sort out. Certainly Andy developed a great partnership with Gerard Wiekens. They complemented each other so well.

Wiekens was as strong as an ox. Massive thighs. The first day he came in we all said he had a touch of Arnold Schwarzenegger about him! He was very strong. He would shield the ball so well nobody could get round him. Gerard was a good lad too. He took his time to settle down and learn English but he never ever let anyone down. Towards the end of his career he showed that he was good enough to play in the Premier League comfortably, marking Ruud van Nistelrooy out of the game in a 3-1 win, the last league derby at Maine Road.

Andy was tough as nails. I remember one morning in the treatment room and Kevin Horlock used to have a bit of banter with him. Usually they were quite friendly together but on one occasion Andy made a joke to Kev and with lightning speed Kev turned the joke back on to Andy.

This resulted in Andy chasing Kev round the treatment room, finally catching him and putting him in a headlock until Kev's face went blue and three or four of us who were in there at the time getting strappings and treatment had to jump on Andy to get him off because Kev went a little bit limp. We actually thought Andy was going to strangle him! It's a difficult one for a manager I suppose. Where is the line in dressing room banter and when should he react and how should he react?

Andy was just one of those characters though. The fans loved his all-action style and he scored a thunderbolt at Oldham which is still talked about now.

Millwall away was a memorable occasion. We took a couple of thousand supporters down there for a midweek game and they were all kept in for over an hour while the Millwall fans went round smashing up their own area and fighting the police.

Lee Bradbury got us out of jail with a last-minute equaliser. We were a big draw for them and City and Millwall had some history from the late 1980s when City's Guvnors firm gave them a surprise at London Bridge. While the City fans had mainly dismantled their hooligan groups, Millwall of course still had a very active one. Inside the ground they had lads everywhere and it was very intimidating for the players.

They made monkey noises at all our black players and they smashed up our team coach outside. I never liked going there even when I went with QPR later in my career. Even big lads like Danny Shittu who could obviously look after himself never relished going to play at Millwall away.

After the game Joe Royle had to say it was a good job we didn't score a second otherwise he would have feared for the safety of our players. Theo Paphitis, the Millwall chairman at the time, then went on the defensive and said, 'If a handful of youngsters going on the pitch intimidates Joe Royle's players they should go back to kindergarten!'

The truth of the night was that there was violence, there was racist abuse of our black players and for their club to appease it was wrong in my view.

There were many low points. The fans have talked about their experiences at these places over the years but for us players it was the same. I'm a Blue, I was wearing the shirt and I felt it.

Lincoln. Wycombe. Darlington in the FA Cup on the Friday night. The humiliation of playing in the first and second rounds of the FA Cup and the possibility of going out before all the other big teams had entered the competition. Our games were televised so there was no hiding place even then.

What was weird was that even through we were struggling, we still had an awful lot of players going out of the club on international duty to play for their countries. We were 'rubbish' yet had internationals all over the show. So you would have weeks where people weren't always around the club and with games coming thick and fast perhaps we weren't able to work on things as much as we'd have liked to.

Tactics-wise we seemed to alternate between playing five at the back and a straight 4-4-2. Much of the time we were playing without wingers so my job was to bomb forward as much as possible and provide a bit of extra pace and width and help with the attack whenever I could, then get back and cover defensively.

There were perhaps a number of reasons why we couldn't pick up our form and while certain players had their contracts bought out and were released by the club, that still left a hell of a lot of others and in cup games some of these would get a run-out as if to keep them in the shop window.

The quality of football in the league was mediocre at best. The pitches were terrible. The referees were terrible. We never seemed to get anything from the refs. Tackles from behind would go unpunished from the opposition near enough every game and we would get players sent off for absolutely nothing.

Then there was the Auto Windscreens Shield game against Mansfield. It had a low turnout but then again it was a competition nobody at the club cared to be associated with and the fans certainly didn't have anything to prove to anyone in the media about their loyalty. A run in that competition would have just proved to be a distraction and would have affected the promotion charge.

The *Daily Mirror* did a feature on it, showing empty stands and sticking the knife in. Kicking the club while we were down. The following Saturday the fans invaded the press box and sought out the reporter from the *Mirror* who had to lock himself in a cupboard. The City fans never forget.

Let's just put on record here that the average home attendance that season was 28,261 and that in a season where we spent half of it outside of the play-off positions. Where were we when we were shit? The City fans WERE there when it counted.

Darlington away was a night I remember well. We had to take turns to get changed in a Portakabin. It was windy, it was wet, it was cold, it was dark, and yet a real hardcore of around 1,000 fans made the trip up north to their old ground at Feethams. It was a small horrible pitch. The pitch was like a bog. You could hear practically everything the crowd were saying and they were lambasting all of us. It was probably THE worst night in terms of the crowd going nuts at us. Everything about it was a confidence killer.

Willie Donachie was shocked by the anger from the travelling City fans as it was the first time really they had shouted over to the dugout too and with Joe, Willie and Asa there they had three guys who really knew the club inside out. To feel they were starting to lose the trust of the supporters was a shock to the system personally for them.

It prompted a robust defence of the squad from Willie both in the match programme and in his weekly column in the *Manchester Evening News*. He used the events of the Darlington game, where we just scraped a draw, to appeal to the supporters to look into their hearts and give the players a break.

'I feel there is too much negative criticism of the team,' he said. 'Maybe it stems from years of failure. We have the most loyal fans in the country and their support is unwavering but there are too many critics who want to emphasise the black side of every thing.'

The realisation that we might not get out of this league was something that would put fear into players and fans alike.

I played in the defeat at York when we dropped to our lowest ever point. OK, we were actually 14th after a game at Notts County in September and we were 'only' 13th after York and four points above the relegation zone after that match. With that game being in December it's kind of regarded as being the club's real lowest point.

These were real low points in our history. Everything was ten times harder than we thought it was going to be. The home teams would do all sorts to unsettle us. They would turn the hot water off, or turn the heat off. On the pitch they would be straight into us every game so we couldn't play, disrupting our rhythm and making us look like prima donnas and soft touches. It worked.

Lincoln City knew how to rub salt into the wounds. They beat us 2-1 in a league game and if beating us wasn't good enough for them they had to show a complete lack of class by refusing to shake hands with our bench and snubbing proper football men like Joe and Willie.

Macclesfield Town. For a club used to playing derbies against United the prospect of a derby against the Silkmen, who had only recently come into the Football League under Sammy McIlroy, was the ultimate statement of how far the club's standing had fallen.

There was actually a lot of pressure on us to win the game. The ground was packed to the rafters and even though half of the home end was filled with City fans too, the home fans sensed an upset. I think at one point they hit the bar. It was a tight and tough game and we scored a late winner through Shaun Goater. God bless that man. There was a pitch invasion from about 60 or so City fans, half joy, half relief.

We had two teams in that league who had real financial muscle – Fulham and Wigan Athletic, backed by Mohammed Al Fayed and Dave Whelan respectively. No one dared to say that Fulham or Wigan were 'ruining football' though. Oh no, that was all good for the game! There was always a danger that somehow we might miss out. Apart from that opening game against Blackpool we were never at the top of the league.

During that promotion season of 1998/99 I played at left-back much of the time with Lee Crooks slotting in at right-back. My preference was to play on the right but you are just happy to play for the manager and Lee was a dependable lad who also scored an absolute thunderbolt of a goal at Chesterfield which brought the City fans on to the pitch again. The grounds were like that in those days. City fans seemed to be on the pitch every week!

If you look at the crowds of all the teams, when they played us it was either their record attendance or their biggest crowd in years. We were certainly good for the bank balances of those clubs, that's for sure, and when we were struggling in mid-table some of the chairmen of those teams must have been rubbing their hands with glee that we may be visiting them again the following year.

We turned the corner from Boxing Day onwards. Wrexham away was a 1-0 win and a scrappy goal from Gerard Wiekens. It was one of the worst games of football I have ever seen or played in. It was a joke. About 4,000 of our fans behind the goal had to endure that. We were literally sat in the dressing room laughing with relief about how shit we had all played.

Maybe something clicked that day. Maybe the fear went. We knew we could play rubbish and still win. Stoke were next at

Maine Road in front of a full house and we came from behind, probably the first time all season we'd done that. All of a sudden two quick wins and six points made the league table start to look a bit different. At the end of the Stoke game you felt that the clouds were starting to slowly clear. There was a bit of fight back in the place and the fans were responding. Looking back, those games gave us a bit of momentum for the rest of the season.

We were picking up points in the home games now as we moved into 1999 and we were finally beginning to feel comfortable handling the expectation levels around Maine Road again. Overall we were playing a lot better but before Christmas both at home and away we couldn't turn those draws into wins. Ultimately those two points dropped here and there would mean we would fall short in terms of automatic promotion. We weren't helped by bizarre refereeing decisions such as Kevin Horlock at Bournemouth who got his cards for 'walking aggressively'!

Millwall at home saw a riot and a continuation of the bad feeling between the supporters from earlier in the season. Millwall brought a large mob up and as soon as Paul Dickov opened the scoring it was the start of missiles being flung over from both City and Millwall fans in the North Stand and from a pocket of Blues in the Kippax lower who tried to charge the away fans.

For ten or 15 minutes it was just nuts inside the stadium, total anarchy, and we all just played on. We went from 1-0 to 2-0 and then 3-0 and with every goal that went in the Millwall fans became even wilder.

Burnley away was another memorable one, a 6-0 win and a night the City fans really started to love the big man Shaun Goater up front. When he scored his hat-trick he ran straight into the City crowd and they all rubbed his head and patted him on the back. The Goat had started to bond with the fans in a big way and once he felt the love his confidence went through the roof. What a love affair that would prove to be.

We were involved in the very first televised pay-per-view game against Colchester. The City end was packed as always. No matter where we went they were there. Shaun scored again, this time with a stunning volley. The fans respected him as they could see he was putting in a shift every game.

A home defeat against Wycombe Wanderers really put a nail in our coffin as far as finishing in one of the top two places was concerned. We could have let that affect us and destroy our season but mentally we had time to get adjusted to the fact we would be in the play-offs and with the club never having been in any kind of play-off before it was at least going to be something exciting, a chance of Wembley and a chance of promotion.

So it was Wigan first who we had beaten twice in the league, 1-0 on both occasions, and both had been close games. The first leg at Springfield Park had been an awful match on a waterlogged pitch. Now bear in mind we were the poor relations of the two in those days and it was Wigan who had the rich owners pumping money in.

Multi-millionaire Dave Whelan had done a fantastic job getting Wigan up through the leagues. They were a very ambitious club and this was to be the last ever game at Springfield Park before they moved to the new stadium. A historic occasion all round then. A further 10,000 fans watched the game on a big screen back at Maine Road.

Wigan went ahead in the most ridiculous of circumstances. From the kick-off the ball went out for a throw. Tony Vaughan threw the ball across to Gerard Wiekens and both he and Nicky Weaver left it for each other. Up popped pocket dynamo Stuart Barlow who simply caressed the ball into an empty net.

That was a nightmare start, 13 seconds it was. Half the City fans weren't even in the ground. Half of them were still climbing over the wall or forcing the entrance open to get in! To be fair to the lads we kept a very motivated and purposeful Wigan side quiet after that and kept ourselves in the game. It was a tense and scrappy game all round.

At half-time, while walking in to the tunnel Andy Morrison had a fight with big Eric Nixon, who was on the Wigan Athletic staff at the time, and it was like the Royal Rumble in wrestling with bodies flying everywhere and those two were throwing people out of the way trying to get at each other.

Things were getting thrown about and police were trying to get involved – it was one of the craziest things I'd ever seen. I literally got on to all fours and just crawled on the floor in an attempt to get back to the dressing room! I'm not sure exactly what sparked this off. Probably just two passionate guys and a very tense semi-final situation with so much at stake. It was a good job they didn't have tunnel cam like they do on the City website these days.

Time was running out when we found the equaliser. Michael Brown put an inviting ball into the box and Dicky lost his man at the near post and fired home. We were told to stay positive and get forward from full-back. We kept plugging away and got our reward eventually. The final score was 1-1 and the away goal gave us a very slight advantage going into the second leg.

The return game against Wigan at home was played four days later. It was a superb atmosphere. If you looked at the stature of the two clubs then and the history at that stage there was no comparison but at the time it was a very even game. We had the away goal which meant that we didn't have to panic if the early goal didn't come. We could play a more patient game.

There was so much depending on that result. It was tense but very loud. Incredible. I think the crowd had decided there was no way we were going to lose this. There would probably had been a riot had we lost, they were so up for it. City got to the FA Cup Final in 1981 and lost. Then there was the daft Full Members' Cup Final against Chelsea in 1986. It was a trip to Wembley but it didn't really count. The fans were completely starved of success so any trip to Wembley, lower-league play-offs or not was a long time coming for the City fans.

Wigan complained about the goal but as everybody could see it was a perfectly good one from Shaun – in off his nipple, they all count. A massive outpouring of relief came as the fans poured on to the pitch, covering every blade of grass, and carried the players down the tunnel. Manchester was going to have a big day out at Wembley.

9

I'M DREAMING OF A BLUE WEMBLEY

THESE days Wembley is like a second home for Manchester City but back in 1999 it was the first time in a generation for many people going there and they had a famous song they used to sing at Maine Road, 'Wembley, Wembley, it's a shitty place in London that we're never gonna see.' Hard to believe that now. Well...we all had to pinch ourselves but this time we were all definitely going to Wembley!

If memory serves right we had two or three days off straight after the semi-final to just let everything settle down and settle in. Emotionally it was a great journey we'd been on. We played 48 games in the league and the play-offs and the final massive 49th game to come would shape the future of the club and probably our own individual futures.

There were 11 days between the second leg of the semi and the final so when we picked up training again we had about a week's good training in the build-up to the game.

Looking at where we are now, with the great stadium, great players, trophies and being known worldwide as the only football team to come from Manchester, it's hard to put a figure on what promotion out of the third tier was worth to the club. As we all know it was a key moment in the club's history but at the time we had to try and treat it as just another game.

For the likes of David Bernstein and his board of directors the stakes would have been at their highest. Nobody could have stomached contemplating another season in that old Third Division but that's what defeat would have meant.

As soon as City reached Wembley the papers talked about how many Blues would be making the trip down. Gillingham wouldn't bring many surely so the rest of the ground would be for City. As many as 50,000, 60,000, who knows? A record turnout from one club's fans?

There was consternation when the FA said the clubs should get close on equal numbers for the game – 37,000 for City and 34,000 for Gillingham. City's average crowd that year was over four times larger than Gillingham's. These were the days when supporters used to queue up outside the ticket office, right throughout the night for games like this.

Gillingham were letting their season ticket holders buy four extra tickets each. After that their tickets still went on open sale. No doubt there were a few hundred 'City fans' with addresses in the Kent area suddenly getting tickets. City sold out of their allocation quickly and there was a bit of criticism in the press about how the tickets had been released. Some City season ticket holders missed out.

I was bringing a full minibus of family and friends down as they all managed to secure tickets. Play-offs or not, Wembley is Wembley and playing there is a proud moment in any footballer's career.

Joe Royle didn't want the media circus coming to Platt Lane disrupting the players' preparations in such an important week. Down at Platt Lane it was very open, the fans could come down and shout over at you while you trained and anyone at Gillingham might have been able to read our tactics or get information leading up to the big game.

For many of this particular City squad it would have been the first time they would have ever got anywhere remotely near the twin towers of Wembley as it was then so Joe had us train at Maine Road on the pitch all week with the only spectator being dear old Stan Gibson who couldn't wait for the players to get off 'his' pitch. Maine Road, like Wembley, was a very wide pitch but that wasn't the reason why we trained there. It was just to give us some privacy.

We had done well in the two league games against Gillingham that season. Firstly we had drawn 0-0 at Maine Road back in the autumn when we weren't really playing well and we were in the middle of that sticky spell. Often we would end up getting frustrated at home in the early part of the season with opposition teams happy to put ten men behind the ball, park the bus and say, 'OK, now it's over to you to break us down.'

We had a good win down at Priestfield as we beat them 2-0 in the April sunshine during the run-in when our confidence had finally picked up. Terry Cooke and Kevin Horlock scored the goals on that occasion and that win at Gillingham actually ended their impressive seven-month unbeaten home record in the league.

Nicky Weaver also broke the record at that game for the number of clean sheets kept by a City goalkeeper in a season, taking the record from Alex Williams. The defence was settled and working well as a unit by now. So it was felt that going into the game we were the better team and Joe and Willie both made that point over and over to us in the run-up, saying whichever 11 they would end up picking to go and face Gillingham we would be a better 11 than anything they could put out.

I felt sure that I would be playing at Wembley, probably at left-back, but we wouldn't actually be told the team until very near kick-off. I was in good form personally and in terms of injuries had enjoyed a trouble-free season. Ian Bishop was the main injury doubt and would go on to have treatment in the hotel right up until the last minute. He had told the manager that he was fit to play but he hadn't been guaranteed a place in the starting 11 – he just had the guarantee of a place on the bench at the very least.

Also in the week leading up the game the club brought in a motivational speaker called Bill Beswick who was giving us tips on how to approach the match and think about what we wanted to achieve. That aside though, it was all about keeping things as routine as normal and I think they did a pretty good job in that respect. The managers never focused on the Gillingham players, it was always all about us. What we were going to do, how we were going to play and how we were going to impose ourselves on them.

We travelled down on the day before the game and our hotel was actually overlooking Wembley itself. You could see the twin towers out of the window. That's when it hit home what an important game it was coming up in the morning. I had managed to sort out all of their tickets for friends and family before coming down so that way I was able to deal with football-related matters only once I was down in London.

I'm not sure who was in charge of the music on the way down but it was a lively coach, relaxed and full of good banter with the card school in full flow as per usual at the back of the coach. On arrival at the hotel Kevin Horlock was up to his usual tricks, going up to reception to get everyone's room keys then purposely handing out the wrong keys to everyone so they couldn't get access to their rooms!

I was rooming with Kev as normal so we weren't affected but I did think, 'Oh no Kev, we're at Wembley, can't you leave it alone just on this one occasion and have a normal night?' There was no such thing as a normal night with Kev though.

In the morning we had breakfast then went for our walk around the hotel as we normally did at away fixtures in those days to stretch our legs. It was a drizzly morning if memory serves and there were a few City fans dotted about wishing us well.

We had an early lunch then boarded the coach. We were given the team line-up that morning – Nicky Weaver, Lee Crooks, myself, Andy Morrison and Gerard Wiekens. Terry Cooke, Jeff Whitley, Michael Brown and Kevin Horlock. Shaun Goater and Paul Dickov up front. Bish hadn't made it and had to make do with a place on the bench.

As we approached Wembley we were overcome by the hordes of City fans lining the streets with their flags, their scarves and their clenched fist gestures up against our windows. Lots of the blue home shirts and seemingly even more of the yellow and black away shirts which we would be wearing that afternoon. You could see how much it meant to them. In two hours we'd be playing for them at Wembley.

City fans had the tunnel end and our coach was parked up at that end of the ground. As we got off the coach our dressing room was on the right-hand side of the tunnel and I looked down the tunnel to see if I could get a glimpse of the pitch. There was a kind of ramp leading up to the pitch but all you could see was a bit of the seating and the sky but you couldn't actually see the pitch. Inside the dressing room, Chappy was putting the kits out and there was my shirt with my name on.

Suddenly I felt we were getting focused on football once more and not just the occasion.

Willie kept our warm-up exactly the same on purpose. Getting into little clusters of seven or eight players and having a game of head tennis or two-touch. We didn't fear Gillingham but we certainly knew they possessed a threat up front in the shape of Robert Taylor, who was a goal poacher, and Carl Asaba who liked to put himself about everywhere. In tandem they would provide a stern examination for our defence.

I don't remember much about the team talk other than Joe reinforcing the message that we were better than the team we were facing and we should just let our quality show.

Out on to the pitch we went to a then-capacity crowd and were met with a sea of flags and a wall of noise. Even though approaching 80,000 were inside the old ground, which was a record for a play-off final at this level, the first thing you did as a player when you were lining up was to look out for any friends and family.

It had been raining all day, heavily at times, and the pitch was very soft underfoot when we kicked off.

It was a cagey opening period and on the whole the approach play from both teams was quite poor but we slightly edged it in terms of quality of football. I was pressing down the left wing at times with Jeff Whitley earmarked to keep hold of their main man in midfield, the old general himself Andy Hessenthaler, who would later go on to become their manager.

We could have had a stonewall penalty in the opening few minutes but it was not awarded despite a blatant handball in the box. Maybe the referee bottled it because it was so early on in the game.

Much of our good work in that first half came through Terry Cooke and we were having the better of it in all areas across the pitch at that stage. Against the run of play Asaba did have the ball in the net momentarily but seconds later it was ruled out for offside then moments later I was up the other end connecting with a great ball from Michael Brown and I narrowly missed out after my diving header just crept the wrong side of the post. It was 0-0 at half-time.

Into the second half we were looking for that goal to break the deadlock but Joe decided upon a double substitution and although this decision was later widely recognised as having 'changed the game for City' the switch initially seemed to fire up Gillingham instead.

Andy Morrison picked up a knock and was replaced by Manchester lad Tony Vaughan. Secondly Ian Bishop finally came on at the expense of Michael Brown. Browny was disappointed to be taken off.

With big Andy missing perhaps Gillingham sensed they could get something and seemed to find a little more space, then ten minutes from time the deadlock was broken. Five minutes later Taylor had added to Asaba's opener and the Gillingham fans were going insane. Maybe they just couldn't believe it. We certainly couldn't and our fans were in shock but yes there it was, a quick look up at the scoreboard which read Gillingham 2 Manchester City 0.

To put into perspective what a bad situation this was, the other lot from Trafford had just won the treble earlier in the week.

After years of disappointment and let-down the least the City fans expected was promotion from the old Third Division through the play-offs.

Apparently at this stage Noel Gallagher had walked out of the ground. The papers the next day had a picture of him with the catchy headline 'Don't walk off in anger'.

I've got to be honest. My first thoughts at this time were the same as those of the supporters, 'Oh christ, not another 12 months in this league.'

To be honest, none of us knew who would be staying with the club had we not gone up. Further cutting of cloth would have definitely had to have taken place. We thought we'd run out of time. For a few thousand of our long-suffering fans it was game over and they were heading for the tubes and the trains.

We kept playing though. Kevin Horlock pulled one back with 15 seconds of normal time to go. Too little too late was the general feeling among the support. Scoring one so late made it even more torturous. Similar to the Aguero winner against QPR in 2012, where two goals were needed and that second one was the decisive one, the first one, by Dzeko – just like Kevin Horlock's – so often gets overlooked in the grand scheme of things but it was to prove absolutely vital.

The board went up and five minutes of stoppage time went up on the board. A huge roar came from our end and we all believed again.

We kept asking questions of Gillingham. Ian Bishop was driving us on and keeping us ticking over. He was prodding and poking and looking for gaps. He had been sold by Howard Kendall all those years ago as he was viewed as a 'luxury player' but now in the club's darkest hour, he was the one player that might just keep this club alive.

In all fairness to the third substitute, Gareth Taylor, he was involved in both of our goals, linking up with Shaun Goater and in the case of the second goal, what a fantastic strike that was from Paul and an amazing celebration on his knees across that wet Wembley surface. We were back from the dead. The boys in blue never give in.

The whistle went to take us to extra time. We had got the momentum and Tony Pulis had taken Asaba off while they were in the lead, so for them it was a case of parking the bus throughout extra time and clinging on for penalties.

We felt at that stage we would definitely go on and win it. I actually felt we would win it during extra time but we didn't seem to create the chances during the extra half an hour. The pitch was very heavy on our legs and you just needed to look around to see how it was taking it out of everyone. About five minutes before the end of the second period it looked and felt as though both sides were now settling for penalties.

So many people have come up to me over the years and said, 'Richard, I never expected you to take a penalty for us at Wembley.' The truth was though that I always knew I was taking a penalty if I was still on the pitch at that time.

After we got through in the semis we practised penalties at the end of each training session. Obviously it doesn't and never can replicate the match conditions and the pressure you would get at Wembley but it can show a manager who has the confidence to step up and take one, who has the best records in practice and it also gives you a chance to perfect your own technique.

I would always choose my side and stick to it. I would usually aim for the side netting to the left of the keeper. Before we went down to London, Joe pulled five or six of us aside and said we would be the main penalty takers should it come down to penalties. I always felt confident that I would score mine before the game. Then as soon as the final whistle went to signal the penalty shoot-out my mind began to turn to the fact I was going to have to step up and take one.

The penalties were to be taken at the City end of the ground and Nicky Weaver whipped the fans up into a frenzy

– 'Weaver,Weaver, Weaver' bellowed the supporters in response.

First to go was Kevin Horlock who stepped up and scored. We had a lead. Then Weaves saved the first Gillingham penalty from Paul Smith and it was bedlam. The confidence soared. Next it was Paul Dickov whose penalty hit both posts and stayed out, a measure of revenge for his good friend Vince Bartram after Paul had scored the equaliser against him right at the end of injury time. The confidence dipped again so we went over to Paul as a group and consoled him.

Unbelievably Gillingham missed their second and we seized the initiative again. Terry Cooke then scored a great penalty and it was 2-0, a bit of breathing space. There was lots of pressure on the next Gillingham penalty but this time it went in for 2-1.

Now it was my turn. It was a long walk from the centre circle to the penalty spot and I had seen Kev walking slowly before his penalty. I couldn't understand why he was choosing to walk so slowly. I just wanted to get there, take mine and get off.

So I ran up to the box, put it down on the spot and waited for the whistle. My legs had turned to jelly and my mind had turned to mush. My only thought was – stick to what you have practised and don't deviate from it. Another three or four seconds and I think I'd have passed out. I looked over and the ref allowed me to take it. In it went off the bar and I had finally broken my scoring duck for the club – and what a way to do it, at Wembley of all places.

The celebration said it all really. Pure relief. Then a feeling of pride. My arms were in the air and I was kissing the badge. We were almost there. Weaver saved the next one and there it was – promotion! We got swept away in a tidal wave of noise and passion, Nicky was doing his own personal lap of honour around the stadium and in fact if Andy Morrison hadn't tackled him near the halfway line he'd probably still be running now. We had done it.

You felt for the Gillingham players, of course you did. It was a long, hard season and they were shattered. We were singing and dancing on the pitch. I had got the daft blue wig on and we were walking up those steps to pick up a bit of silverware. It felt surreal. An hour beforehand we were dead and buried and dead men walking. It was one of the best feelings of my life.

Eventually we boarded the coach to make the short return journey back to our hotel. The place was packed full of City supporters. As we got near the door we had to get out and we were all mobbed while walking into the foyer. I was looking round to see my nearest and dearest. It was incredible but I was trying to take it all in.

After a quick drink the City squad split up, some staying with family in London overnight for a meal, and the rest of us – around 15 or so – going back up to Manchester on the same night. Although we didn't get blind drunk on the way back, we did have a very merry time with lots of banter and we just looked at each other saying, 'Did that really just happen?!' Chappy was up and down the aisle of the bus doing his daft impressions all night and making us all laugh.

We stopped off again near Altrincham for a quick scoop and we found a pub still half-full of City fans even though it was late. Soon we were back on the bus to Maine Road where some of our cars were but I had no idea how I got home from Maine Road or who might have driven me.

Over the next few days there were a couple of parties which was nice because it meant sharing your success with people you have achieved it with. A barbecue at Paul Dickov's house was followed by a party at Kevin Horlock's where he had ordered a smoke machine and a dry ice machine and you walked in unable to see anything.

Kev was just there, hyper as usual, bouncing on his feet non-stop for two hours and flinging his arms in the air like a nutcase. We just laughed and laughed and laughed. The club was reborn and two things were evident – there was a real bond between the players and the bond had also returned between the players and the fans.

10

MOVING ON UP

THE success of Wembley was still fresh in everyone's minds as we reported back for pre-season training. We had somehow scrambled out of that division and were now one step away from the Premier League again. It felt as though we had broken the cycle of doom and negativity and were looking in a forward direction again.

Just what would have happened to the club had we not won promotion against Gillingham, who knows? Chris Bird even said just that during stoppage time while it was still 2-1 to Gillingham. Going up in that fashion was arguably better than going up as runners-up, as Walsall did, because we were able to give the fans a bit of glory and a good day out. The only downside I suppose was a very short break as the play-offs had meant an extra two weeks at the end of the season but we were on a roll, we had turned it around and all worked hard to achieve something positive.

Now we all wanted another taste of success. As a group we couldn't wait to get back to pre-season with Joe, Willie and Asa, a big contrast to the feeling of dread the previous year and being flogged to death at HMS Torpoint.

We were full of confidence and by keeping the nucleus of that promotion team together and by adding a few astute signings we felt in the camp that we could give it a real go in 1999/2000.

We made some good additions and we signed players, some of whom had played at the highest level such as Mark Kennedy. 'Super' Mark Kennedy as the fans christened him was a great lad who had been at Liverpool and Millwall. A very good player with a sweet left foot and he came in and settled in with the group almost immediately…in other words, he liked a drink!

Joe and Willie must have felt even when we dropped into the third tier that the plan would still be back-to-back promotions and Premier League football in two seasons. Joe was talking up a promotion tilt and saying we could be aiming for the play-offs but as the season progressed they must have felt they could have got us over that line just as they did all those years ago at Oldham.

Wolves at home in the opening game meant a clash between the two biggest clubs in the league and Robbie Keane's winner brought a defeat but it was still a good performance. A goalless draw at Fulham was notable for the dismissal of Andy Morrison after a tangle with Stan Collymore. Then the goals flowed the following week at home to Sheffield United and very quickly we found our First Division feet.

After an injury-free year the previous season I had one or two little problems but this was to end up being one of the most enjoyable campaigns of my whole career.

We enjoyed some good early wins against the likes of Nottingham Forest and Bolton Wanderers, big names compared to some of the teams we were struggling so badly against the season before. The belief was back.

We were more than holding our own against the bigger teams in the division. The ground was full as it was in the bad days yet the pressure seemed to be off. Wembley meant a new start for everyone and the home games were a real pleasure to play in that season as we fed off the energy of the crowd.

We played Southampton in the League Cup and I had a tangle with Mark Hughes where I ended up being stretchered off and staying overnight in hospital. Hughes was sent off for an elbow and the City fans let him know what they thought about him. We lost 4-3 in an epic game at The Dell which was televised and gave a reminder to a nationwide audience that we could trade blows with more lofty opponents. It also showed that Shaun Goater was more than capable of finding the net against Premier League opposition.

Then there was a game against Port Vale when Ian Bishop scored two goals, his first goals for the club in almost a decade, which put him on a hat-trick.

Bish was different class for us as well. He could play in a telephone box, he was just that comfortable on the ball. He could play in a pair of slippers. He was one of those players who could just keep the ball, keep us moving forwards and you could give him the ball when he was marked by two or three people and he'd still come out with the ball and keep it for us.

Not just that but he was one of those guys that when he received the ball his first thought would always be to get his head up and look for which forward pass would be on. You'd very rarely see Bish passing it sideways or backwards. Playing it short, playing it long, popping up in the hole and being so positive in possession, he only had one mindset which was to play it forward. He made the game look easy. Bish kept us ticking over and his quality helped win games to give us a platform to build upon in the early part of that season.

It would turn out to be a great finale for Bish who could have stayed on an extra year at West Ham and picked up his testimonial but he wanted to come back because he had unfinished business with the club. Bish made the game look so easy.

Particularly on Saturday 23 October I was in love with the crowd and they were in love with me. 'One Richard Edghill, there's only one Richard Edghill' was the chant ringing around Maine Road after I opened the scoring, my first ever City goal from open play, against a Blackburn Rovers side who on paper had a Premier League feel about them. I came off the pitch grinning like a Cheshire cat. You couldn't take that smile off my face. The main reason I scored against Blackburn was my fitness level. I was getting forward all the time that season.

We just carried on the momentum from the season previous. Joe brought Danny Granville in who had been on Chelsea's books and Danny had Mark Kennedy in front of him. The way we played, Mark was sometimes typecast as a luxury player but he had the ability to make things happen and he was a real asset for us because of his near-perfect delivery when crossing a ball, usually putting things on a plate for Goater. Mark worked hard off the ball though as part of the team and as part of Joe's plan you had to be willing to do that side of the game. Mark did and his contribution was immense.

Two months and five days later it was all change again. During the Grimsby game at home, which we ended up winning, I made an error which gave the visitors an equaliser and the next time I was on the ball I got some boos from the crowd. Loud boos. I got some fan mail that week from supporters who felt I had been unfairly singled out.

The time after that when I touched the ball the majority of the crowd cheered to drown out any further boos. The media picked up on it but although I was hurt about it I just played it down and used it as motivation to better myself. A football field is an unforgiving place especially with 30,000 tense supporters surrounding you. There is no hiding place, you just have to play through it and move on.

That was a great season to be playing in front of the home crowd but if there was one player who was going to get a bit of stick it was still usually me!

Christmas approached and despite a couple of wobbles we were still up there. Excellent victories over our main promotion rivals Charlton and Ipswich made the media sit up and take notice and the Ipswich game was the battle between the two best young keepers in England, Nicky Weaver and Richard Wright. Nicky gave a masterclass that night and was rightly given the man of the match award.

It was a new situation for many of the squad. A promotion race to get back to the Premier League where the club belonged so there was so much at stake. We were getting close to the Premier League again so it was hard not to think about it. We weren't the best team that season but we had great spirit and we had the momentum from the previous season so it was important that we bounced straight back up while we could as if we missed out there was no guarantee of getting up the following season. So close you could feel it, touch it, taste it and yet still so far away.

It was hard not to take note of what the other sides were doing – the likes of Charlton, Ipswich and Birmingham – especially in the run-in after Christmas when it might have played on your mind a bit but we had a strong management team who kept our feet firmly on the ground. We were getting the usual amount of media attention but this time the stuff being written about the club was all positive.

Kevin Horlock was another great character in the dressing room for us. As you must have gathered by now he was a very funny guy indeed and always playing jokes and pranks. Around the time of the the millennium celebrations he was suspended for the game we were playing so he came into training with a shot glass full of vodka or whisky and took part in training with his glass still in his hand.

Joe made him sit in the dugout while we were still doing the warm-up round the pitch and let him heckle the lads, saying we were all shit, but he was a great character. I roomed with Kev for two or three years on away trips and training camps and he was just an unbelievable character.

He would always be doing things to wind me up. For example, once he came out of the shower with nothing on and said, 'Come on then Edgy, whose bed am I sleeping in tonight!'

Another time he got me into loads of trouble. All the lads had to attend lunch after training at Maine Road just to try and get everyone to eat together and bond as much as possible.

We were waiting up in the kitchen. Layachi Basckouchi was the general manager there and he used to do all the general jobs at Maine Road, especially player liaison. Because he spoke lots of different languages he would always be heavily involved with players behind the scenes.

Kev dared me to grab hold of his tie while we were waiting to get served. The lads had been waiting ten minutes for their food so I grabbed it and then as soon as I did, Kev went for it as well. We started pulling Layachi over the counter in the kitchen. Then he grabbed hold of my jumper and it ripped from my shoulder all the way down to my waist.

Layachi went a bit flush in the face and we thought he was having a funny turn but everything was all right. I still speak to him now…but Kev used to dare people to do things and then they'd get into trouble.

Jeff Whitley was another one always getting me into trouble. He would end up in the back of a car with a girl after a night out and then promise her he was going to ring her the next day. 'What's my name did you say? Err... Richard Edghill...I play for Manchester City.' Monday afternoon I would get quizzed by some club official about where I had been when I'd probably been sat at home watching *News at Ten* or *Question Time*!

Come to think of it I was in trouble with Joe on more than one occasion and again, it wasn't my fault. One night I'd been out to Nemesis nightclub in Rochdale with my cousin and a couple of others and we were just keeping ourselves to ourselves in one of the little alcoves.

Then a couple of lads, who were absolutely paralytic drunk, recognised me and came over and started having a go at me. At this point my cousin stepped in to do the talking to keep me out of it. Even after offering to buy them a drink they were still being aggressive.

The next week the club got a call from an enraged fan who said that I 'abused' the guy, told him to f*** off and being a season ticket holder of 12 years he wanted me to be sacked. Another time they got a call saying myself, Michael Brown and Jeff Whitley were all walking down the street in Oldham, smoking weed. You'd then have the police coming down to the dressing rooms to take statements. It was laughable, we hadn't even been out there.

Christmas also meant doing some good deeds and as players we would go to visit the children who would have to spend Christmas in hospital. It was always a pleasure and never a chore.

Back on the pitch and into 2000, after a disappointing defeat at Sheffield United where Michael Brown scored the winner we headed out to Lanzarote for some warm weather training. At least that was the official line!

'We'll freshen the minds as well as the bodies,' said Joe to the media, claiming the squad were grafting hard. 'Nobody should run away with the idea that we are on holiday. We are not.' As it turned out we won promotion that season as everybody knows so perhaps letting your hair down in the sun was all part of the plan.

On the coach going to the hotel Joe got on the microphone and said we were going to do some work and also relax but there was to be no drinking until the evenings. We would meet every day at 6pm and then after that the time was our own.

We got there and we had a few hours to kill until our scheduled get-together where we would assemble and have our evening meal.

We had a mooch round and there was nothing much on the complex of note, just a little Spar-type shop. The pleasantly surprising revelation was that the shop was packed full of every type of beer, wine and spirit you could imagine plus all manner of cigarettes!

Looking up and down the shelves it was all the usual snacks, crisps and chocolate bars you'd find at home, the place was full of goodies. We couldn't believe City had put us up in a place like this and not checked there was a place selling booze on site.

All the lads were walking around but after a while we all seemed to congregate near this shop where everyone seemed to be egging everyone else on to make the first move and go in and buy something. We were like a group of schoolkids you see hanging outside the paper shop waiting for someone older to walk past so they could go and buy cigs for them. After a few minutes Bish took the bull by the horns. 'Fuck it, I'll get a few bottles,' he said, and off he went.

A few minutes later he came around the corner trying to shove this shopping trolley which was piled high with every brand of beer and spirit you can imagine! It was so heavy at one point it took four players to push it up a slope. Just as Bish was closing in on his room at the hotel, Joe Royle and his staff came round the corner and caught Bish trying to get all the booze back to the hotel. 'You never did have good timing did you Bish,' said a horrified Joe before going off shaking his head.

The 6pm meet arrived and one by one the players same in. Me and Kev Horlock were two of the early ones. Others arrived in dribs and drabs. What was then blatantly obvious was that everyone in the room was either very merry or totally blind drunk.

Everyone was giggling like naughty schoolboys under the impression that no one would notice what state we were all in. Joe and his staff arrived but we were a few players short. It was Jeff Whitley's birthday and everyone kind of agreed that Joe wouldn't mind if we had a drink because of that. By 6.15pm we were all sat waiting then in came Paul Dickov and Tommy Wright, who didn't really have a clue where they were but they offered up an apology to the boss.

Moments later followed Jeff and Mark Kennedy wearing sarongs, sombreros and both with cigars in their mouths. Both of them were absolutely drunk out of their minds. The whole place broke down in laughter. People were on their knees it was so funny. I'm not sure Joe saw the funny side though. Jeff patted Joe on the shoulder. 'I fucking love you gaffer, you're fucking brilliant,' he said which kind of took the sting out of it and was one of the highlights of the whole trip.

By the sounds of it this Lanzarote trip was just one big piss-up. Well, actually it was. Yes, we did some training but the lads were on the sauce all the time. We really bonded on that trip and whether or not it was a deliberate ploy by Joe to say no drinking before the evening meal, knowing full well it wouldn't happen… the result was real camaraderie among the squad.

After the meal the lads all met in a side street near the hotel as planned. There was a tattoo parlour right opposite. 'I'm going in there,' said Kev. We all sat outside this place having a drink, saw Kev going in and waited for him until he came back out again.

'Look at this boys,' he said. 'I've got a tattoo with my wife's name Karen on, she'll be so pleased I've done this for her.' And there it was, the dedication to his wife with a love heart on his shoulder. None of us realised until the morning that the guy had spelt Karen wrong and Kev, now sobered up, hit the roof.

He had to wait till the following evening until he could go back in and he demanded they remove this tattoo. They said they couldn't do that so he had the heart bit extended to cover the part of the word that was spelt incorrectly. By now it just looked like a big awful mess, he just had a big red blob all over his shoulder. I think he's still got that tattoo and I am not sure his Mrs was too pleased to see it either!

Another feature of the Lanzarote trip was the regular visits to Chicago Rock café bar which we found out was 20 minutes away in the resort of San Antonio (not the Ibiza one), that backed on to Puerto del Carmen. A couple of nights there was a convoy of seven or eight taxis taking us all out to the resort and taking us back again.

Tommy Wright was rather the worse for drink one night and ended up having a row with a doorman who wanted to chuck him out. Big Tommy wouldn't listen and wanted to stay. We'd been in there for hours, the drinks were flowing, we were all belting out songs and there was a big red Cadillac in there and everyone would be taking turns to get plastered in there.

This time it turned ugly. Tommy and this doorman were wrestling on the floor and the police were called. Our convoy of taxis had a nice police escort all the way back to the Lanzarote Beach Club Hotel Complex.

Another time I was in the back of a cab with Jeff and a couple of others players. Jeff was flicking the taxi driver's ears all the way in the car on and off for literally ten minutes. Suddenly the driver stopped the car in the middle of the road and locked the car doors. He then went in the boot and came alongside Jeff's window holding a big baseball bat. We got the message and after a couple of minutes of trying to calm the driver down he agreed to finish the journey.

Some of the behaviour on that trip wasn't very clever I have to admit. I suppose if you were a City fan who had just spent the last few years going to York, Colchester, Northampton and these other places and saw what the players were up to you'd probably never want to go again but the players needed to let off a bit of steam and at the time it was the done thing.

One thing was for sure in those days; there were no real cliques in the dressing room. We were all on a similar level wages-wise and we were all grafters which is what Joe wanted. These days players would have a posh Christmas do. Back then we'd have all just gone in Sawyers on Deansgate and got ratted together.

That league was really hard but running ourselves into the ground during pre-season really paid off. We were a very fit team. Everyone was now knuckling down and even those on the fringes of the first team were simply desperate to be involved. We looked a decent outfit, solid at the back, and had some very good results that season.

I remember Fulham at home where I bombed forward and crossed for Shaun Goater. I was enjoying my football so much.

Shaun was incredible that season. We may not have had the best players in the world but we got our results through work-rate and Shaun deserved all his plaudits.

Joe Royle's ethics were based around working hard and closing people down, and we had a different kind of option with Mark Kennedy out on the left.

Half-time team talks – most managers give different ones. Brian Horton was quite calm at first but as the pressure of the job increased more and more he used to come in and bollock you, screaming loud. He wouldn't scream right in your face but he would kick the big silver skip we put our kit in, and launch the tea cups everywhere. You would really feel his wrath.

Joe in comparison was quite calm most of the time but he would go nuts occasionally, probably when he felt he had to. Willie would just say how it was, no airs and graces, he would just be brutally honest with you.

Joe knew how to work the players. He knew when to put as protective arm around a player and also when to lay into them like Huddersfield away.

I was having a bad game and Jamie Vincent was getting the better of me out on the wing. We went in 1-1 at half-time but we were all disjointed and I myself knew I was underperforming. I was out of position, the game seemed to go too fast for me at times. It was horrible.

Joe went round the room one by one at half-time, getting his digs in but mainly doing it in a non-personal way. He didn't make an idiot out of you in front of everyone although he did say to me, 'Edgy…we're playing in fucking blue tonight.'

I don't know what it is sometimes that means you don't bring your A-game when you cross that white line. You can go into a match thinking about all sorts of stuff. The conditions. The floodlights – often the position of the lights can impair your vision, something happening in the warm-up not quite right, it could just be anything.

It's all about getting under a player's skin and motivating them if they drop their standards by even one or two per cent.

Alan Ball was a shouter and a screamer, so was Kevin Keegan. By the end of my career I had got to the stage where I had worked under so many different managers that I just ended up switching off.

Players would generally keep a straight face if one of their colleagues was being laid into at half-time but in those days – the days before tunnel cams and the like – there would have been the odd comment as you walked back out on to the pitch. If I was having a bad time on the pitch my usual way of getting my confidence up again was to make a crunching challenge and make my mark on the game (and the opposing player).

March 2000 and going to Forest to steamroller them 3-1 in front of a huge City following stands out in my mind. Robert Taylor was with us by then, he'd joined from Gillingham and was forming a useful partnership up front with the Goat. It was also providing a bit of competition for Paul Dickov at a time when we needed goals.

We didn't – and couldn't – play well every week. Some games we brought our A-game and other times we didn't play well but we kind of found something from somewhere to get us over the line.

Norwich at home was a game we won after being stuck at 1-1 going into the last few minutes. At home to West Brom we were behind until very late on and pulled something out of the bag to win 2-1. That game ended a streak of seven without a win which, looking back, cost us the title. We weren't at our best but against West Brom we held our nerve and showed some character. We kept playing and playing and things came off for us.

Richard Jobson scored an important goal at Stockport. Jobbo was great, even though he was coming to the end of his career and he wasn't that mobile. His influence was still there, he wasn't a big talker but I think with his performances and his presence he did really well for us. He could read the game so well. He had great timing and a calming, organising influence.

Danny Tiatto was another good lad. A crazy Australian, he would go out on lads' nights out and just fall over drunk – I think he damaged his collarbone twice doing it! Danny was a good player though and was quick and strong for his size. He didn't say a lot – I think in fact he only said about three words in all during his time. I think he was underrated in the eyes of the press but the fans certainly appreciated his all-action style.

We had so many unsung heroes in that side. Nicky and Shaun were the fans' favourites and kind of the star players but our real strength that season was the team unit as a whole.

Gerard Wiekens was a very good player. Solid. In training you couldn't get the ball off him. Paul Dickov was one of those as well in training who would kick seven bells out of you and still be your friend afterwards. He just wanted everyone else to work as hard as he did.

I thought we had a good mix at that time in the dressing room. I think it worked really well for us, work hard play hard, and if there was the odd occasion when people came to blows on the training ground it would all be forgotten about by the time we got changed.

I have mentioned Kevin Horlock a few times and said how insane he is but he was also just a fantastic guy to have around the place. For a midfielder Kevin had a tremendous scoring record and was a good penalty taker. OK, he wasn't that mobile but he worked his socks off. He suffered a bad injury one year but even so not many would match his scoring ratio. The goals he provided from midfield were invaluable.

Jeff Whitley had a great season that year, full of work-rate. Andy Morrison was a colossus at the back until he picked up an injury which forced him out of the run-in. Lee Crooks gave me competition for the right-back slot. We called him 'Trigger' after the *Only Fools and Horses* character. He wasn't the brightest but he had bags of character!

We were just a dedicated group of lads who all decided to put everything into it for two years solid to get us back where we belonged.

Birmingham at home at the end of April was a must-win game against Trevor Francis's team who were always in and around the play-offs. Robert Taylor wasn't prolific for us but he provided some much-needed competition for places up front at the right time and he bagged the all-important winner on this occasion.

It was a night of celebration where the fans came on to the pitch. We had one foot in the Premier League and Ipswich were playing at Charlton the next day. We all went down to London for the PFA awards night hoping we'd be up by the time it all started. Ipswich pulled off an amazing 3-1 win at Charlton which meant the gap was two points going into the final game and we could be caught if we lost at Blackburn and Ipswich won their last game. Charlton were already up so maybe they were already 'on the beach' so to speak and perhaps the result wasn't a surprise after all.

There were some comments in the press from the Ipswich camp saying they thought it was all a bit arrogant from our side when they saw the players celebrating with supporters on the pitch when we hadn't actually got promoted yet. It was hard to dampen the fans' enthusiasm. They had been to hell and back and so had the players. Joe took the sting out of it by saying the fans just wanted to show their appreciation for the players' efforts. However if we didn't get promoted, boy would those scenes come back to haunt us.

Blackburn away was an incredible day. No City player or fan will ever forget that. Our team bus struggled to fight its way through the masses of Blues outside the ground. As we passed The Fernhurst pub it looked like the whole of Manchester had turned out to cheer us on. They were waving their flags, banging on our windows, looking into our eyes. Police estimated 15,000 Blues made the trip that day including a few hundred on the hill outside the ground!

The City fans were certainly in all areas of Ewood Park and we knew it would feel like a home game for us. We just couldn't let these great fans down.

Building to Blackburn was very nerve-wracking, much more than any other time that season.

Joe Royle had made me captain and this could be the day that I led the club back to the promised land. The players used to say I was Joe's dad because he always called me 'Edgy son'!

I wasn't a ranter or a raver, I wasn't one to go round handing out rollockings but I would lead by example. I think Joe saw leadership qualities in me plus I knew the club inside out, I had shown loyalty to the club, I was known to all the players and all the staff. I think Joe quite liked the fact I had been around the club for a long time. I was a reliable character for him, I wasn't a massive boozer, I didn't get into trouble and knew what it would mean for the club to get back-to-back promotions. For me personally it would mean everything. It would be about righting wrongs too.

Of course I had scored in the earlier fixture against Blackburn and that goal I think proved that what Joe was trying to do was coming over. Shaun scored a bagful of goals with the help of Mark out on the left and to have promotion in our own hands on the last day of the season was great. But having to get a result at Ewood Park against the likes of Damien Duff, Matt Jansen and the rest of them meant it was no foregone conclusion.

I always felt at home at Manchester City. I'd been there since the age of 12, I always felt it was my club and to be asked to be captain of the club I love was an honour I shall never forget.

The nerves were starting to get to me before the Blackburn game. We were just 90 minutes away from the Premier League but should we drop into the play-offs there would have been no guarantee about going up.

I was thinking about everything we had put in over the last two years to get to this stage. I was in the dressing room trying to remain calm and focused. I wanted to ensure that I left nothing back in the dressing room, I wanted to make sure I was taking everything out with me on the pitch.

The game itself was incredible and it was obvious the nerves got to us all that day. Blackburn were in total control and we could have been 5-0 down before we equalised. I think they hit the woodwork on four separate occasions. Then you realise it's still only 1-0 and you begin to feel 'hey, we're still in this' and it could be your day after all.

Good old Shaun equalised for us and from that moment the belief and confidence swung from Blackburn over to us. What a ball across the six-yard box it was from Kevin Horlock to set him up.

Then we had the own goal from Christian Dailly and some breathing space. We'd have to let in two goals not to go up. We never looked back after that. Ipswich were winning but it didn't matter. Goals for Mark and Dicky were fitting rewards for their efforts that year.

I was playing down the right, next to the Walker Steel Stand. It was half and half between our fans and their fans in that stand and I could see ours creeping closer and closer to the touchline. You could feel the atmosphere and the pitch invasion was imminent.

The City fans who had been outside on the hill were drifting in and the other ticketless City supporters who had been watching in the pubs around the ground were now streaming in. As they opened the gates towards the end it was brilliant really because people who hadn't been able to get in originally also had the chance to share the celebrations.

The fans in the stand were doing the conga and they were getting ready to invade the pitch. When the whistle finally went I was the first player to get engulfed by that great big tide of humanity swarming on.

They were everywhere; on the pitch, in the dressing room, and those lads with their arms around Joe Royle in the directors' box were all mad Blues from Higher Blackley I am reliably informed.

It was just a great sight to see the pitch totally covered with our fans. And to be there looking out at and seeing fans and players celebrating as one, all singing City songs together after the way things were 18 months earlier, the them and us situation between fans and players, it was just unbelievable.

What a great bunch of players they were. And best of all we gave the fans their pride back. We came back to Manchester and had a reception at the Midland Hotel. We were back in the big time and pitting our wits against the best teams in the country.

But first…celebration time!

11

I WANNA BE ADORED

TWO years previously I had waited for the fixture list and looked at the teams we were facing; Blackpool, Wycombe, York, Lincoln. The fixtures came out this pre-season and the schedule looked a lot more normal again. Manchester United, Liverpool, Arsenal, Spurs. We were a big club and we needed to be playing other big clubs.

I was so looking forward to this season and being back in the top flight after years in the wilderness, years in the lower leagues, years of injury. Looking at the fixtures we had a home derby before Christmas, early trips to Elland Road and Anfield and the three opening games involved a trip to The Valley to play Charlton, the team that had pipped us to the title the season before, followed by Sunderland and Coventry at home. It was surely a chance to get some points on the board early on.

We played one pre-season match in Northern Ireland and one against Drogheda in the Republic a couple of days later. Joe Royle had said, 'Right lads, this is an important trip…no one's drinking,' and after the Drogheda game Bish had gone up to Joe and said, 'Boss, the lads are itching to have a drink.' Joe flipped, saying, 'Can you not have one night without having a drink?' He went mad.

I think Nicky Weaver was still up and drinking at 4am and we were flying back home around 6.50am. He wasn't the only one but he was particularly rough. It got to a stage where it was too late to go to sleep and the players might as well have stayed up and gone straight to boarding – so that's what they did. A load of players were turning up at the airport still drunk and stinking of booze. Coffees and paracetamol were everywhere as soon as we'd got through check-in.

The club were trying to secure the signing of Ugo Ehiogu for most of the summer but Middlesbrough had more financial clout than us at the time. Coming through the door was a bit of firepower in the form of George Weah and Paulo Wanchope and Joe also brought in Steve Howey and Richard Dunne to bolster the defensive unit. They were a couple of hard-working professionals but boy, did they like a drink as well.

Joe fought had to break the drink culture at the club and in the end the press would use it as a stick to beat him with, printing the bar bills from trips abroad. Joe also brought in Laurent Charvet so I had some competition at full-back.

George Weah certainly was a strange one because I'd only ever seen him on Channel 4, on *Football Italia*, playing for AC Milan. He'd previously won the World Footballer of the Year award and for me as a 25-year-old lad to see him walk into our changing room after everything that had gone on in recent seasons was just unbelievable.

George had a presence about him. He was very friendly and I think he had one of those dodgy passports because in training he didn't try too much, maybe he was older than he said he was! He also claimed to be a lifelong City fan having seen them on telly in the 1970s. He must have been the only City fan in Liberia, that's for sure.

His first appearance in a City shirt was in an embarrassing 4-1 defeat at Stockport County in a friendly. We looked yards off the pace. Weah scored but he didn't look fit though.

Willie used to have a tough training regime on a Monday morning to catch out some of the lads who would have been out drinking over the weekend. On a Monday we'd do a fitness session warm-up where we'd do three or four laps of the training ground. Willie would always be at the front and he wanted players to keep up with him as he was such a good athlete. He certainly didn't want players trailing behind him.

I think George came in, did the first lap on the first training session and decided that was enough and started walking, which Willie was probably a bit upset about.

George added other qualities though to our dressing room. He was a marquee signing but it gave the group a boost knowing he was in the squad and he would contribute in training and engage with the other lads. However, he played a prestige friendly in Marseille the week after he joined us and ended up signing for them within three months!

Willie did a lot of fitness stuff. He was determined to keep the squad fit. The training was there for everyone but if you didn't fall in line and do the work then you weren't going to play and I think that's what happened with George. He played 11 games for City but only lasted the full 90 minutes on three occasions. Shaun Goater started getting the nod ahead of him so Weah went to see Joe and asked to terminate the contract.

Weah owned a football boot-making company in Italy and he'd come in with these different coloured boots with him every single day. Chappy the kit man got a few pairs off him and that was his way of joining in the dressing room banter.

The club had made it clear they were breaking the existing wage structure when they sanctioned the deal to bring George to the club. There was a core of us who had escorted the club through the divisions and were on a certain level of wages. We knew that the next group were coming in on much more but to us it didn't really matter that much. We weren't bothered what they were on because we knew it was a completely different level of salary, a level we could not have achieved through agent negotiation anyway.

There was never any talk of salaries as far as I can remember in the Joe Royle era. I would know that Laurent Charvet for example would be coming in on more money than me but it was up to me to accept the challenge and show the manager I should still be first-choice at right back or anywhere across the back line. I could play as a right-back, a left-back, as a wing-back, in a three across the back or as one of two centre-halves. Coupled with my previous Premier League experience I felt I would have enough to offer the club as we moved back into the big time.

With the club more financially sound than at any period in my time there players would be coming in on big money but again I saw that as motivational and I wasn't going to start rocking the boat over it.

Shaun Goater was another one. Players would come in during his time like George Weah, Paulo Wanchope, Robbie Fowler, Nicolas Anelka and Jon Macken, yet ask the fans about who they remember with most affection out of that lot and the answer will be the Goat every time. That's the unique thing about Manchester City. Fans recognise when a player has his heart in the club.

I had a measure of respect from the other players. In terms of being captain material I was never a shouter or a screamer, my game was about having a quiet determination to succeed, and there was an imbalance in that there were bigger personalities in the dressing room. However, I felt my career was definitely on the up again.

The first game of the season was at Charlton, a battle of two newly promoted clubs. We rolled up at The Valley. 'City are back' was the cry from our end yet 90 minutes later we were sat in the dressing room disheartened after being thumped 4-0. In all truthfulness it could and should have been double that. We used a new system of three centre-halves and three in midfield with me and Danny Tiatto as wing-backs. Spencer Prior, Gerard Wiekens and Steve Howey were the three at the back.

The next game was the following midweek. Peter Reid's Sunderland were the opposition but this time it was a very exciting match and a morale-boosting 4-2 win. Sunderland had won their opener 1-0 against Arsenal and may have been regarded as favourites but Joe went with the same team that were played off the park at Charlton and said, 'Now you lot rectify it.' It was a superb response from the boys.

Peter Reid and Niall Quinn were coming back to City and there was a real buzz in the air. It was a really brilliant atmosphere for our Premier League homecoming. I was so proud to lead the team out after all that had gone on at the club, and what a game it turned out to be.

We were two goals to the good early on through Wanchope and a rare strike from Alfie Haaland and we were creating chances by using a mixture of short and long passing. We were competing well but maybe the system was allowing the opposition to play as well. Quinn and Kevin Phillips brought them back into it at 2-2 but then instead of crumbling we found another gear and saw them off 4-2 with Wanchope going on to complete a hat-trick.

During that Sunderland game, I had a dust-up with Don Hutchison and he made a very unsavoury remark towards me. We had to be separated on the pitch and the crowd were loving my passion, shouting my name in support, but they didn't know the full story of why I had lost it.

At the time Hutchison didn't like a tackle I made on him and he said something quite distasteful in response. I tried to get at him again in the tunnel but was stopped from doing so. Hutchison tried to apologise after the game but I didn't want to know. These days there are so many cameras in the ground that what he said would have been picked up but at that time he got away with it.

I felt reasonably confident going into the next game which was 'that' Coventry match. On paper it looked winnable but the day certainly didn't pan out as I thought it might have done. Like my debut at Wimbledon and the occasion at Leeds where my cruciate went, Coventry at home is a day forever etched in my memory, a game that shaped my career and was a key moment in my life.

I was always taught by Tony Book and Glyn Pardoe, two great full-backs, to train the way I would play. That way you would leave nothing in the dressing room come matchday. I always gave 100 per cent to the cause, I was totally wholehearted and when I put that blue shirt on nothing else mattered.

Being an apprentice and coming through the system I was never regarded as a star turn among the support. However, all I wanted to do was play for my club – Manchester City.

These days all footballers are well paid and even during my time at the club some of my team-mates were just here for the money and wouldn't know the first thing about the shirt they were wearing.

Not all of us were paid megabucks. Star signings have bad games but because of the investment, because of the wages, the fans normally cut them a bit of slack. Some players may get booed and they couldn't care less. I was really upset when the crowd turned on me at the Coventry game that season but I learned to live with it and let the sad feelings I had about it go.

Other footballers have had similar experiences and those reading this will know where I am coming from.

We started poorly that day, we were lacklustre and I don't know why. We'd won one and lost one beforehand and the performance and character displayed against Sunderland had given everyone a shot in the arm. Any game in the Premier League was going to be a challenge though.

Perhaps there was an expectation among the supporters that the Coventry game would be a walkover. The truth was we were still the new kids on the block in Premier League terms. This was our third top-flight game in four years and we were still finding our feet.

Nicky Weaver was a good keeper who had been on a great learning curve while moving through the divisions. At one stage he looked like he might go all the way with the national side. He certainly didn't lack any confidence. He gave us a good base to work from.

There was a lot of pressure on Nicky with comments in the media about how he was going to be worth £15million! Nowadays I think there would be more protection and more advice for an up-and-coming talent like that.

In the promotion season he kept so many clean sheets he took the long-standing record from Alex Williams. The amount of saves he made won us so many points we would have lost otherwise. The back four would work consistently with him in training and the move which unfortunately resulted in an own goal against Coventry was one that in training I would have headed back to the goalkeeper 50 to 60 times in a week and there would have been no problem whatsoever.

Weaves would always stay on his line. He was a great shot-stopper and whether I would head or chest the ball back to him I would know exactly where he would be, such was our understanding. As it happens on this occasion I headed it to where he normally would have been but Nicky had moved so of course the ball crept past him and into the net.

On this day it was strange because the ball held up in a swirling wind and for some reason it took a long time to come down. Weaves came out slightly away from the side he was covering and as it came down I'd instinctively headed the ball back to where I thought he would be.

A few minutes later we had a corner and I stayed back but we lost possession and were caught on the counter-attack almost immediately. Craig Bellamy was on the ball and I was shepherding him away from goal but he managed to find the net from an outrageous angle which made it 2-0 and put me under the spotlight even more.

I was then booed for the rest of the half until the teams went off. Every touch of the ball I had I was booed by a section of the crowd. As we walked off at half-time the booing was very loud. It could have been meant for the whole team but for me it felt like they were singling me out and getting on my back.

I was mentally strong as a player and as a man generally and although I was very upset about the booing I was still prepared to play on in the second half. In the dressing room Joe just said to me, 'Are you all right son?' and I said yes but he took me off for my 'own protection'.

I wanted to answer the crowd back but I had to rise above it and roll with the punches. I had walked off the pitch with a massive weight on my shoulders but I wasn't getting the chance to atone for my errors which meant that weight simply stayed there.

Driving away from the stadium we had the fans' phone-in on the radio and my dad who was driving had to turn off in disgust as I was being pulled apart by people ringing in. It was a sickener and I was overwhelmed by so many negative responses. Of course I could see where some of the comments came from but to be honest it just hurt.

I could have done with a chat about it with the staff afterwards but I was just told that I was being stripped of the captaincy for the foreseeable future.

Looking back I honestly don't think I could have done anything different. The high swirling ball took ages to come down. Weaves moved position. I'm not blaming him, not at all. What I am saying is it was just one of those things that happens in football. We work hard in training to avoid them but sometimes fate determines otherwise.

There was a similar incident with Joe Hart and Matija Nastasic away at Chelsea the other year. A communication mix-up. I had two bad incidents in one game. I was moving Bellamy away from goal as we are taught to do but he still managed to score and make me look bad. Bellamy was only 21 then.

In the 4-3 derby defeat at Old Trafford in 2009, where Michael Owen scored that late, late winner, Bellamy scored from a similar angle when Rio Ferdinand tried to usher him away from goal. Keith Curle did the same with Ryan Giggs when he tried to show him the corner flag and Giggs put it in the top corner in the 1996 Maine Road derby. You get days like this in football.

I wasn't one for banging on a manager's door and making demands like some players I could mention. I was more the sort to just get my head down, work hard in training and show the manager that I was worth my place and that sooner or later he would have no option but to bring me back into the team.

You'll all remember Gary Neville's clumsy back-pass in the derby when he fed the Goat at Maine Road. He had a nightmare that day and was substituted. He was dropped for the next game but he got a run-out after coming on as substitute and was soon right back into the mix. As a player if you've had a bad game you kind of need another outing quickly to make amends, to put things right. I never got that opportunity after the Coventry game. I was stuck on the sidelines, out of the team, out of the squad, out of the equation.

Joe and I never really talked about it much. We weren't doing any better in the league once I had been dropped and I was tremendously frustrated seeing other players just picking up their wages while I was chomping at the bit on the sidelines. Joe said publicly that he wanted to take me out of the firing line for a while. However after a couple of months there was still no sign of me regaining my place in the first team.

Fan mail. Yes there were star players at the club during my time and I was never regarded as a star player myself but I used to get lots of fan mail. I kept loads of letters – hundreds of them. I mostly got mail whenever I was booed!

On the whole the City fans were very supportive when I had my bad times. A minority would have a go at me on a Saturday and by the Monday the club would have passed on tons of emails from fans wishing me well, followed by letters in the post. A few times, Julia McCrindle, who was the manager's secretary at the time, would be in touch saying, 'Richard we've got a load of emails for you that have come to the main email address at the club. I will forward these on to you.'

After a few weeks without a sniff of a return to the first team Birmingham City came in with an offer for a month's loan and

I needed the football so I went down there to St Andrew's. To be honest they were kind of a sleeping giant. Trevor Francis was a nice guy and they had a decent enough group of lads but I wanted to be back at City, back in the Premier League, and my heart wasn't in it down there because I never really wanted to be there in the first place.

So back I went to Manchester and by the time I returned George Weah had walked out on the club and the home form – always the key to a newly promoted team staying up – was abysmal, culminating in a massacre at the hands of Charlton over Christmas. Laurent Charvet, my replacement, was substituted before half-time during the 4-1 home defeat. I had a phone call afterwards to say I was back in the fold for the New Year's Day game which amazingly was Coventry again, this time at their place, and at last I had a chance to make amends.

I received a tremendous ovation from the travelling fans which was great for me personally, and we lost the lead to end up with a 1-1 draw. I was pleased with my own performance and now I had the shirt back it was my intention to retain possession of it indefinitely.

After Coventry we then faced Birmingham in the FA Cup at Maine Road which brought me up against some familiar faces having been at St Andrew's just a few weeks earlier, and after that we had another big game in the league against Leeds United.

We played well against a star-studded Leeds team but a couple of late goals made the scoreline look bad. After that Joe had decided he wanted to go back to a 4-4-2 system and it would mean I would be dropping out again. It was a real sickener.

I would be going to the games when I wasn't playing and watching from the main stand or from one of the boxes in the

Platt Lane End. I would leave the ground ten minutes from time so as not to be spotted.

After a while it was apparent I wasn't going to feature again and there is a game that season where the City crowd were full of their gallows humour. The lads were playing Arsenal and were 4-0 down at home in just over half an hour. That same night I didn't go to the game. I was at a venue within earshot of Maine Road watching one of my brothers playing in a non-league match. I went to the car at half-time to hear the score and was dismayed to hear the contest had been over so quickly. I could have been playing against Thierry Henry and the rest of them and I felt quite bitter about not being able to win my place back in the squad at that moment.

Soon after this game the players regained a small measure of pride when they held United to a draw at Old Trafford. Steve Howey was on the scoresheet for City that afternoon. This was also the game where Roy Keane and Alfie Haaland clashed and the feeling inside the club was that Keane did intend to 'do him'.

Ian Bishop's time with us came to an end. He felt we could play our way out of trouble but Joe had settled on a formation which involved playing Gerard Wiekens in midfield and Bish felt his chances would be limited. When you look back at the progress the club made under Joe it was fantastic and the City fans backed him to the end like they back all our managers. Playing in three different divisions in three seasons was a tall order. When you are promoted to the Premier League you are promoted straight into the relegation zone.

The media hung Joe out to dry, citing the drink culture, and it's true there were players there who got away with a lot. In this current era of Twitter and other forms of social media it would be interesting to see how much they would have got away with. One paper printed the receipt from a bar bill from one of the trips abroad so you have to wonder how they get access to this type of information. It would have built a case to justify sacking a manager. Of course clubs don't normally sack a manager without having a replacement of sorts in mind but with Dennis Tueart upstairs anything was possible in that regard.

We were back in the lower leagues almost immediately and once again facing an uncertain future. Then along came my old pal Kevin Keegan.

12

CHEER UP KEVIN KEEGAN

WE were relegated at Portman Road after losing to Ipswich and immediately the speculation started in the press about a change of manager. Joe Royle was then fired after the last game of the season against Chelsea.

For the third campaign running the last home game had seen a massive pitch invasion. Unlike the previous two years though, the game against Chelsea was technically abandoned when City fans from the North Stand first went on to the pitch then made their way over to confront the Chelsea fans and a mass brawl ensued in the stands.

We were out of the Premier League and Joe was replaced by none other than Kevin Keegan who was taking his first job back in club football after the England debacle. This was probably my most problematic time at the club.

The fans were ecstatic that we were getting such a famous name as manager. Hundreds of them gathered outside the main stand in the late afternoon sunshine to welcome the former England boss.

Even though Keegan had become a figure of fun for the London-based media, the fans on the forecourt were full of hope and expectation. Keegan had revived Newcastle and the City supporters hoped he could revive another sleeping giant in the shape of their club.

Keegan had a football relationship with Dennis Tueart. The press had lampooned him as the 'failure' England manager who walked out on his country in their hour of need just as he had walked out on his 'beloved' Newcastle United. He had a reputation for being a quitter and with City being a club known the world over for having a managerial merry-go-round, the press wondered how long he would last at Maine Road. The rollercoaster was about to start all over again.

When he came in he said everyone at the club would be given a fresh start. I'd seen a lot of managers come in and give good speeches on day one. It was a new slate but I was now into the final year of my contract and sooner or later the issue of its renewal would surely come up. In came Stuart Pearce, Arthur Cox and Derek Fazackerley. They said the lads who had been out in the cold in previous months would be given a chance to at least prove themselves.

Keegan also mentioned that the drinking culture at the club had to stop. He had heard all about it and had inherited this issue and said the first thing he was going to do was break it up.

Richard Dunne was probably fined more by Keegan in the first two months of the new manager's reign than any other player in the club's history! Dunney, bless him, was always late and coming in the worse for wear. Keegan even stopped Dunney from receiving a man-of-the-match bottle of champagne at one point.

Nicky Weaver was one who liked a gargle. So was Stevie Howey. When you are in football you live in a bubble. There are a number of reasons why players fall into this trap. Their upbringing. The stability or perhaps the lack of it in their private lives. You come to this point in your life where you have money and fame but you may not necessarily have had the education or had the right advice in order to be able to deal with it. Or for others drink could just be a way of handling stress.

My great friend Jeff Whitley was brave enough to go public with his battle with alcoholism and it's a battle he has won 100 per cent. Jeff was a former ball boy at City like myself and all he wanted to do was play for the club he loved.

It took him years to confront his inner demons and to actually realise and confess that he was an alcoholic. Football is a very macho environment though and perhaps at a certain time someone asking team-mates for help might have been seen as a sign of weakness. Jeff went into Tony Adams's Sporting Chance rehab clinic to get the help he needed and never looked back.

It doesn't go on now like it used to do. I think the foreign element has brought a change in lifestyles, a change in cultures. Players now might just have the odd glass of wine during the week. It's a totally different mentality and these days the booze is frowned upon. It's more about looking after your body and trying to be the best you can be all the time whereas back then a great many clubs, in fact a great many of the most successful clubs and national teams, would use drinking as a form of bonding and letting off steam.

Think of Arsenal under George Graham. Or think of the Republic of Ireland under Jack Charlton. One player in the Irish squad said that going to the 1994 World Cup was like going on a month-long stag do. Jack Charlton supposedly had a barrel of Guinness in his hotel room! Team spirit originated from drinking together. That was definitely the case in the 1970s,

80s and 90s and I think it's a good thing that the culture has changed.

Kevin Keegan would go on to break up the drinking culture at the club. He moved people on and changed the mentality of the dressing room during the course of his first season.

We were red hot favourites for promotion and we retained a lot of the squad with the parachute payments from the Premier League money. The idea was to do what Charlton had done under Alan Curbishley – come up, come down but then come up again using the nucleus of that squad. Certainly if we bounced straight back it would be all right. Any longer might be a problem.

It felt a stronger club and a better squad than the last time we were in this league. We also learned as a club from that terrible time around 1996 when we got rid of players but replaced them with inferior ones. With Keegan on board there was a confidence that we could bounce straight back.

The first game of the season was City v Watford, Kevin Keegan v Gianluca Vialli. The two promotion favourites meeting early on. As usual there was a full house at Maine Road and a truly magnificent atmosphere. A 3-0 win was a superb start and confidence among the support was high.

We came crashing back down to earth the following Saturday with a 2-0 defeat at Norwich. I had experienced promotion seasons before and knew how hard you had to work to achieve this but I was in and out of the side during Keegan's first few months.

We had the odd setback in those early fixtures but normally bounced back again the week after. Who now remembers us losing 4-0 at home to Wimbledon that year? It happened though. There was Jon Macken's amazing winning goal for Preston North End from the halfway line which made Kevin Keegan splash out £5m for him.

Carlo Nash, who had forced his way into the first team at the end of the previous season, and Nicky Weaver were now fighting for the number one jersey rather than Nicky being the first name on the teamsheet every week.

This was a squad now who should have been comfortable with being promotion favourites. As it turned out we had more than enough for the rest of the division that year but Keegan still gave out the odd rollocking…but he did things in a weird way!

I remember him doing it while getting dressed, either shirt up pants down or bare chested putting his pants on! Also he didn't always look at the player while giving the rollocking. I'm not sure how much respect he actually got from players. Maybe he thought he was doing us all a favour when he was telling everyone how he would be driving down to the south of France on his holidays in his vintage Rolls-Royce. He is obviously a successful fella but temperament-wise and just on his record alone was he actually a successful football manager?

During Keegan's time we moved the training ground over to Carrington, which was previously land owned by the University of Manchester, and it provided us with better facilities and many more pitches to use. It also provided a little more privacy for the staff than you got at Platt Lane.

Keegan favoured the wing-back system and no doubt had Shaun Wright-Phillips in mind as a long-term option there. Shaun made his debut a couple of years previously and after gaining some Premier League experience would end up being a major asset for the club in this season.

Shaun would go on to show what a successful academy we were developing under Jim Cassell and Paul Power. He soon became a fans' favourite and a truly fantastic player, going on to represent England many times. He is one of the most exciting players the club has produced in recent years.

Keegan liked ball players and brought in Ali Benarbia and Eyal Berkovic so the media speculated on which one of these strong personalities he would have to leave out but he often played both at the same time.

I remember playing in the Sheffield Wednesday game where we won 6-2. Ali was a magician and with guys like Darren Huckerby, Shaun Goater and Paulo Wanchope constantly on the move up front the opposition would always have their work cut out.

Keegan's whole focus in training was centred around doing a lot of work in one v one situations. He wasn't really interested in defenders, he was more interested in working with the attackers and I think most games with the players we had, we could just score more goals than the opposing team. At the end of training he would often make everybody sit down and watch the attackers scoring goals.

He never seemed too bothered if we didn't or couldn't keep a clean sheet. He never spoke about that, or defending well, it was more about attacking, counter-attacking, hitting teams on the break and changing the way we were playing from previous years.

Much of the time we played with a strict 4-4-2 under Joe and things were now changing to a wing-back system with Stuart Pearce often playing as one of the three in the middle of the defence.

With the likes of Ali and Eyal in the squad, I found that playing at wing-back was great. I would double up with one of those players, two guys who could see a pass a mile off. Ali's ball for Wanchope against Sheffield Wednesday proves that particular point. I'd be making runs up and down the wing and that combination worked really well for me. Wanchope turned around in the media afterwards and said, 'Ali sees you when you can't even see yourself!'

That's another thing about being a footballer, especially at a club like City where new managers came in all the time and each one had a different brand of football they wished to employ. As a player you've got to adapt to the way a manager wants things being done.

Adapting from full-back to wing-back was no problem for me. Sometimes I had a winger in front of me, sometimes I'd have no winger. David White played in front of me in the early days and so did Mike Sheron. They were hard-working players who did their jobs. Later on in my time at City unfortunately I did have people who didn't help my cause. People who would not do their jobs, not want the ball and hide during matches and because I had to compensate for them I would get pulled out of position and looked bad myself.

I remember Ali's debut against Birmingham. He only flew in the day before, pulled his boots on and just started playing. He made us tick. I remembered watching him playing in European games for Paris St Germain and thinking what a talented player he was.

Straight after the Sheffield Wednesday game was Coventry away and we lost 4-3 in a mad match. We came from behind three times that day. There was also the time we lost to Portsmouth and not only did Peter Crouch score his usual goal against us but Lee Bradbury scored against us once again.

The thing about that game was it was already our sixth defeat of the season and it was only November. We were off the pace slightly, we were in the pack but not quite hitting top form. There were lots of changes in the team and we did not always have a settled back three or back five if you call it that. After that though we seemed to click and find the winning formula.

Shaun Wright-Phillips was full of energy but I was an experienced player with a good engine and I could play wing-back. I enjoyed playing there. Not only that, after sitting out much of the previous season I was more than happy to compete and fight for my place in the squad.

Away at Burnley early on Shaun Goater scored a hat-trick and I set up two of his goals. I got the man of the match award in the *Manchester Evening News* and they were raving about me again in the papers and on local radio. The player who had been jeered the season before still had something to offer it seemed!

Even though we had the speech at the start of Keegan's reign saying everyone had a chance and it was a clean slate all round, I got the feeling that if you were liked and wanted then you knew that but many of the staff didn't get the feeling they were particularly liked or wanted. I was one of those people and could feel that my time at the club might be up soon. My instincts proved right the day after I got all these rave reviews in the papers after the 4-2 at Turf Moor.

Dennis Tueart popped up in the media to dampen their enthusiasm to say, 'Just because he's had a few decent games it doesn't guarantee him getting a new deal', and I thought that was a very strange thing to say, hardly something to bring out the best in a player.

I remember that Sheffield Wednesday game but it was also the day I got injured again and I thought that might not do me any favours in terms of contract negotiations or cementing my place in the first team.

I damaged the medial ligament in my knee at Hillsborough and up until that point I felt I had trained and played really well in all the league games. Just when I was doing OK and having a little run – and bear in mind to maintain consistent form players need match sharpness and regular football – injuries were forcing me out again until the Walsall match eight weeks later.

I had another little run in the side in the lead-up to Christmas. One fixture was Bradford City at home, a televised match where Shaun Wright-Phillips scored a magical goal and I was back in top form. I was enjoying it as an attacking right wing-back and I felt I was back onside with the fans.

I even went on to the club's website to say, 'I think the reception I received from the fans was brilliant, this season especially I sense a change. They have been great to me. I have had some bad times in the past and some rubbish thrown at me, but I feel they are right behind me now and I appreciate that. It is also good for team spirit.'

I felt that whenever the subject of my contract was finally going to be addressed, at least it would mean I could go into those discussions in good heart and on the back of some solid form.

It was approaching the festive season but how much goodwill was actually in the air around Moss Side? I was halfway through the final year of my contract. On the morning of the West Brom game, on Boxing Day, as I was going through my routine and preparing for the game the secretary Bernard Halford pulled me to one side, handed me an envelope and said, 'Here Richard, when you go up to the dressing room just take a look at this when you've got a moment.'

This seemed strange because I'd already been up to reception to pick up my complimentary tickets so I wondered what on earth this could be about.

There was the bombshell, a letter from the club saying 'Manchester City Football Club are pleased to offer you a one year contract.' This incensed me. Really it was about the way it had been done. OK, I didn't blame Bernard for it. He had been told to do it, Bernard was just doing his job and following orders. That was just the politics going round the club at the time.

It left a sour taste though. January was when I was able to speak to other clubs but it wasn't me forcing them to let me go, I wanted to stay but with a better deal. I spoke with my agent about it and we refused to sign it. I was 27 years old and my ideal solution was to secure a three-year deal. I still had my best years ahead of me in my eyes.

I had one week to sign a contract. It was absolutely ridiculous timing. It was a matchday. West Brom were going well, promotion rivals who had thrashed us 4-0 earlier in the season at The Hawthorns. I was not in a good frame of mind having received that letter probably around an hour before kick-off. I got booked early on for something daft and that was my fault.

However my second bookable offence – for diving – was just a ridiculous decision from the referee and I was off before half-time. With ten men we were happy to take a point.

Both managers said in the press conference that my second booking was harsh and I shouldn't have gone off. We should have had a penalty when Jordao from West Brom took me and not the ball but the referee didn't give it and booked me again. The referee then tried to even it out by booking Jason Roberts for a similar 'diving' offence when his wasn't a dive either.

When I got home I was hopping mad. I would miss the home game against Norwich but I played the next match against Burnley, who were at that stage top of the league. We thrashed them 5-1 after being 4-0 up at half-time. We simply took them apart and put on a great display. Paulo Wanchope scored a hat-trick and Eyal Berkovic and Darren Huckerby chipped in too – and all this after Carlo Nash had saved a Glenn Little penalty when it was still 0-0.

I was definitely playing good football at this time, mainly because the more you play the sharper you become. I was enjoying playing alongside creative players, effective players where, if I made a run and put a cross in, there would be people at the near post, people at the far post, people coming in at angles on the edge of the box to finish the move off.

It was wing-backs again for the New Year's Day trip to Bramall Lane to face Sheffield United. Again Shaun Wright-Phillips was emerging as a great talent here and the 7,000 City fans were in fine voice behind the goal. I'd been there before with City a few years before when the home fans broke into a chorus of 'We hate Wednesday, We hate Wednesday' and the City end all replied 'We hate Saturday!' Going there and showing we were the best team in the league was a great feeling.

Shaun had been impressing in the reserves and was banging on the manager's door for a regular first-team place. I know he could slot in at right wing-back so even though I felt I had the shirt at that moment I knew there was some competition coming through but I relished that challenge. Just like I threw the challenge down to Andy Hill when I was breaking through. Competition for places is always healthy but you always want to play.

We won 3-1 and even had a couple of goals chalked off for apparently no reason. In the end we missed the record number of goals on the last day when Stuart Pearce did a Phil Jones and sent his penalty against Dave Beasant into orbit. However, if those would have stood the record would have gone surely.

We had a big squad that year and competition for places was tight but normally it would be me on the right, Danny Tiatto on the left then three in the middle, with the manager having a luxury of choices, Stuart Pearce, Richard Dunne, Steve Howey, Lucien Mettomo, Gerard Wiekens, Andy Morrison. It was almost like the current era where you have two players for each position.

We were top of the league and next up was an FA Cup match against Swindon Town, which would actually turn out to be my last game for the club. I picked up a hamstring injury that day just as it was going so well again.

Just at this good time for the club there was some sad news with the passing of long-standing groundsman and all-round City legend Stan Gibson. Stan was held in affection by all who knew him. He had a big heart, was a big Blue and his daughter Janice was well known from the souvenir shop.

The papers had been speculating for weeks about four of us who were out of contract in the summer – myself, Andy Morrison, Terry Cooke and Paul Dickov – and whether any of us would be offered extensions.

Yet since August I had tried to raise the topic of conversation with the manager. He spoke to me and tried to keep me involved in anything he'd heard from upstairs…which never seemed to be anything concrete at all. I also never really felt I could talk to him and speak to him about certain things, important things, and looking back maybe he was under orders from the board in terms of the contract situation.

In the papers around Christmas Dennis Tueart then said, 'The manager has not let us know whether he wants to keep Richard Edghill at the club.' All very public, and yet up to this point all Keegan himself could say was, 'I don't know what's happening, the board haven't sorted it yet.' Imagine if I had tried to conduct my business and my negotiations through the media.

Nowadays an agent would go straight in with a director of football. Premier League clubs are run using different models now.

As a footballer you want the best for you and for your family. I didn't feel my 'demands' if you call them that were particularly over the top in any way but those initial positive vibes I had about Kevin Keegan – remember I worked with him when he was involved in the England under-21 set-up – had now evaporated. With Dennis Tueart also involved it really was crunch time as far as the contract situation went and this was to be arguably my key deal but they were playing hardball with me.

I was really angry about it because I felt I had been messed about. It would have been fairer if he had turned round at the very start and just said, 'Look, you are 27 and I recognise you need to be playing every week. There will be clubs out there happy to give you a three-year contract, we acknowledge your contribution and that you love this club but you might want to instruct your agent to get the ball rolling.'

The thing is, City were my club and I was of the mindset that eventually the club would have to come to realise I was a loyal servant whose heart was in the place. Having been part of the resurrection I wanted to see it through to the glory days.

Yes, of course I could have taken the offer of another year and then maybe tried to win another extension afterwards but that's easier said than done when you've been given such short shrift from someone. I felt, in fact I knew, that I was a good professional and felt sure that if Keegan didn't want me then I would be able to get another club.

However I felt the ultimatum was unfair. I'd been in that dressing room with 50-odd pros and seen players come in on massive contracts, play 20 or 30 games for the club then get paid off – in effect they had been paid to leave.

I was 27, wanted some recognition or acknowledgement of my service and the part I'd played in the revival of the club but also to get more than a year as that would offer me some security.

My good friend Kevin Horlock was also offered a one-year deal. He had been there a shorter amount of time, so there was no question for example about a testimonial but nevertheless he took a deal which involved paying as you play and because of injuries he played a few games even in the Premier League, coming on as sub in the 3-1 win over Manchester United, so I can see how the deal might have worked for him.

Nearly a decade on from the Brian Horton episode and here was another City manager employing the same tactics – sign the contract now or else you won't play again!

The one-year contract would have taken me to my tenth year and perhaps a testimonial. So I just asked the question about a testimonial and was flatly refused because the club didn't like testimonials mainly for 'tax reasons'.

Keegan said, 'You think this club owes you a living don't you?' I just said, 'No, I just want the club to treat me with the same level of respect as I have shown the club.'

I wasn't asking for more money, I just wanted a longer deal. I wasn't one of the best-paid players there anyway. He said I had seven days to sign or else the offer would be withdrawn.

The following week I was called back to see Keegan. This time it was a quick meeting. Was I signing the contract or not? I wanted longer than a one-year deal. I didn't think it was a ridiculous demand and still don't. Two years, three years, but not just one year. Also it wasn't me who had set the deadline of one week to sign it. I couldn't possibly sign a contract I was unhappy with. So that was it and the meeting ended.

A few seconds later I had a tap on the shoulder and it was Derek Fazackerley. Keegan had sent Faz to follow me down the corridor just to tell me that from now on I had to train with the youth team.

Faz nervously and sheepishly explained that it wasn't his decision, that he was just passing orders on. Up until that moment I'd had a lot of respect for the boss and his staff but to make the longest-serving player train with the kids was disappointing to say the least. Not just that but Keegan couldn't even be straight with me and have the decency just to tell me to my face like a man. I thought that was very poor indeed but decided to just take it on the chin as I usually do.

I just thought I would keep my own counsel about it and not go moaning to the press. I thought I'd show them I was better than that. I started to realise that perhaps my days with the club that I had grown up with, the club I loved, were soon to be over.

Inside I was raging but as time went on I started thinking maybe I should go and accept a fresh challenge. When you've been at the same club for so long, when City is all you know, the thought of going elsewhere doesn't really come into it but this is where I was now.

My agent at the time talked about some interest from Sporting Lisbon and sent them a tape but we heard nothing back. Maybe I would have been treated better by Keegan had I been on the books of his agent friend Willie McKay!

Willie was the agent who oversaw Joey Barton handing in a transfer request at City at a time when Stuart Pearce had helped him through countless problems. I don't believe that people like Kevin Keegan or Willie McKay ever had any real love for Manchester City but there you go. Maybe if I had played ball and gone along with what these people wanted I would have had a happier time.

I was only on £4,000 a week at the time but I was reading daft things in the papers saying I was on £17,000 a week and after £30,000 a week. They were idiotic stories planted by fifth columnists.

The only time I said something out of anger towards Kevin Keegan was after months on the sidelines after he had discarded me. That season we went up as First Division champions but

I spent my days working with Asa Hartford who looked after the youth team at that time.

Keegan didn't want me around the first-team set-up at all. It was absolutely frustrating but I had to grit my teeth, keep my head down and bide my time.

I'd loved every minute of my time at the club up to this point and now I was faced with this very frustrating episode. Bide my time. Find a deal elsewhere and move on.

In my eyes it was a total lack of respect and I'm not the only player that has experienced that. You can handle a decision if a manager doesn't fancy you but there are ways of doing it. I was being made to feel surplus to requirements.

Time and again I'd seen players come into the club, get to know the staff and then someone else comes in and then they are shown a total lack of respect and everything is made to feel like it's their fault. I'd seen players come in, take the piss out of the club financially then put their feet up as soon as they got a new contract.

Keegan got rid of other staff there because he didn't like them. It didn't matter if you'd been there for two minutes or 20 years, if your face didn't fit you were out. Take Julia McCrindle for example, a loyal servant to the club, the manager's secretary for years and years. She was discarded like a piece of rubbish. That's when I realised Manchester City meant nothing to Kevin Keegan. All Kevin Keegan was ever interested in was Kevin Keegan.

I felt unwanted seeing out the last days of my time at City – out of the picture, away from the squad, a total lack of respect shown towards me.

Then out of absolutely nowhere, the week before the last game of the season Keegan decided to make a bizarre token gesture. He pulled me into his office and said to me, 'You're playing at the weekend' and I said, 'I'm not.' He said, 'You've played a number of games, if you make one more appearance you'll have made the number required to get a championship medal.'

I was flabbergasted. I said, 'After all that's happened this season – making me train with the youth team – you are now going to tell me I'm playing and you think you're doing me a favour… I don't need any favours from you.'

After that last game of the season against Portsmouth all the players came on to the pitch to take the applause from the crowd on their lap of honour. I didn't even attend the game.

A lot of family and friends have said that was a bit daft on my part and maybe I should have gone, shown my face and shown the fans that I was still part and parcel of this great club and wasn't a forgotten man.

Maybe he thought it was a nice gesture, something to ease the conscience. I don't know but I had too much pride for that. Maybe he expected that I would just jump up and thank him for it. Who knows?

I've mentioned Kevin Keegan the person. Kevin Keegan the City manager certainly increased the profile of the club. He ended the drought in derby matches by helping the club to their first victory over Manchester United in 13 years with the 3-1 win at Maine Road in 2002.

However he spent fortunes and it could have been a Leeds situation where expenditure was far exceeding income, especially when wages were taken into account. You'd have to ask the City fans whether they thought the millions and millions he was given to spend were wasted or not. Yes we got into Europe – via the Fair Play League – and then we were promptly dumped back out of it shortly after. By the time he left City in March 2005 how much progress had the club really made?

After I left City I struggled to get another deal and at first I couldn't work out why no one would sign me. There were two main problems here. Firstly the ITV Sport channel had just collapsed so Football League clubs were all letting people go rather than buying anyone new. It was a nightmare time for them. The financial meltdown affected the future planning for all clubs at that level including the recruitment of staff, job security of non-playing staff and also their youth development systems.

The other issue is that if any clubs asked Kevin Keegan for an opinion on me who knows what kind of reference they were getting. Perhaps the feedback they were getting was that I was a 'disruptive influence'. If people were getting this, which was just rubbish in any case, that would have harmed my chances of getting another club. I couldn't prove it but the indications were that there were forces at work trying to dirty my name.

I was never a ranter or raver or a boozer. I'd been club captain for two seasons only recently, culminating in two promotions – promotions which were based on team spirit, hard work and a good attitude so how could I have been a disruptive influence? It was bollocks.

I had 18 months out of the game. I had the odd call from friends but among fellow pros you soon fall off the radar. It's more a case of every man for himself.

I suffered a bit being out of the game. Not out-and-out depression but times when I felt down and I was bottling things up again. I had self-doubt. Why could this 27-year-old footballer not get a club?

I'd always been a strong character with inner determination and possessed a hard work ethic. I was in the wilderness but managers had spreadsheets, they had dossiers, they had scouting reports built up over time on players. Surely I would come into the reckoning for someone at some point. All I had to do surely was keep myself fit and wait for the phone to ring.

I had an agent at the time but they weren't coming up with enough opportunities for me. Wrexham got in touch but they couldn't even offer me a salary – just petrol money! I turned that down because I felt I was at least worth a salary. I had a mortgage to pay and Eve was working so I felt I couldn't just live off her money.

Wigan Athletic were next. Paul Jewell said he rated me highly and asked if I would come for a trial. Again the financial situation for clubs wasn't great and all I had was a non-contract deal. Play and put myself in the shop window so to speak.

I played one game for the Latics in the LDV Trophy against Notts County. I was at right-back and over at left-back was Leighton Baines. Jeff Whitley was in midfield for Notts County. Nick Fenton and Danny Allsopp were also part of the Magpies' team. They had been at City with me.

Perhaps I should have stuck it out a bit longer at Wigan, they gave me a chance. However, I was unhappy with the contract situation and felt I was worth a bit more.

In January 2003 I got a call from Neil Warnock at Sheffield United and went there for a few weeks. I played one game for them and went to La Manga with them for a winter break. Kevin Blackwell was his number two there and I got on well with him. On the Friday, while we were still in Spain, Warnock said he'd like to give me a deal and was in the process of trying to sort me out with something, saying that it was all looking positive. We flew home and by the following Monday I was in his office being told there was nothing there for me and he now wanted to bring in another forward, even though he already had seven or eight on his books already.

Then he said he had a mate who was an agent who could get me a move abroad if I fancied it. Things were going well with Eve at home and playing abroad just wasn't an option for me at that time. Yes, if I was single it might have been a different story but not at this time. Eve was the bit of stability I had in my life.

Next in touch was Graeme Souness at Blackburn to ask if I had got fixed up yet. I said I hadn't, so he said, 'OK, leave things with me.' Then nothing came of it. Something came back about me being a bit of a 'disruptive influence'. I never got an explanation of where that had come from but I tried to reassure them and say that wasn't true at all.

The PFA sends details of all their members who are available on lists to managers, scouts and agents. Nothing came of it. There was no money in the game in the lower leagues. Perhaps I should have done what Michael Owen did in 2009 and put together my own DVD and sent it out to all the clubs to get myself a move.

I also had a trial with Leicester City. There was a good set of lads there at Leicester, good pros full of banter but they could play a bit too. Paul Dickov was there at the time and he was without a car so I used to meet him off the motorway and drive him to training. Tim Flowers was there, and later on of course he was the goalkeeping coach at City. Frank Sinclair, Muzzy Izzet, Matt Elliott; they were all big personalities, people you could rely on.

I liked the set-up there and was quite keen on a move to Leicester at the time but again I got the feeling that politics had played their part. One morning I got pulled to one side. 'What have you done to piss Kevin Keegan off?' said Micky Adams, who was in charge. 'I've done nothing,' I replied. Adams and Keegan had obviously spoken given the closeness of their relationship. The move to Leicester never materialised. By now I was frustrated beyond belief. Not just that, it was demoralising.

Who knows what had happened behind my back. Perhaps Kevin Keegan took umbrage with my comments and tried to show that I would need favours from him after all to find a club. He certainly knew how to alienate players and not just me. Whatever the truth of it was, it was an immensely frustrating time.

13

LONDON CALLING

JANUARY 2002 was the last time I had kicked a ball in anger for Manchester City. In my last league game for them I had helped them reach the top of the First Division, a place they would stay for the rest of the season as they returned to the Premier League with a superb total of 99 points.

They also equalled a club goalscoring record for the number of league goals and would have beaten that with Stuart Pearce's last-minute penalty miss against Dave Beasant. I was certainly good enough to be playing at the top of the First Division and I still felt good enough to be in the Premier League.

Fast forward to August 2003 and I was literally keeping fit just to stay sane. It was all I knew. It was my defence mechanism to deal with the situation. Go for a run. Go to the gym. Have a game of squash. Have a round of golf. Do some weights. Go for another run! Even now I take great pleasure in getting the tracksuit bottoms on and going out for a run. It's good for the mind, spirit and body.

One day I was playing golf at Tytherington with Stuart, my father-in-law, and I always had the phone on just in case. The new season was upon us and I was seriously beginning to lose faith in football. Then, as I was about to tee off on the tenth hole, my mobile rang and I didn't recognise the number.

I had a gut feeling it might be important and said to Stuart that I needed to take the call. It turned out to be Ian Holloway down at Queens Park Rangers. 'Richard, would you like to come down to London and sign for QPR?' At last my luck was changing!

Instead of asking Kevin Keegan about me as so many others seemed to have done, Ollie had asked Joe Royle about me and of course received a glowing reference. I flew down the very next morning and never looked back.

Even though I was on a high I didn't want to just drop everything, I made sure I finished my round before I went down to London. My confidence was sky high again and our team ended up winning this golf tournament. Stuart still has my crystal vase. I haven't had it back since that day so Stuart – if you're reading this I'd like it back please!

I have to say that I enjoyed two super years down there at QPR and I really enjoyed my football there. My good pal Ian Brightwell could perhaps point to something of a similar experience. He was out of first-team football for 18 months also although he still had a club. He joined Walsall under Ray Graydon after spending a lot of time in Coventry City's reserves. As Bob will tell you, when you do start playing again it's like a new lease of life.

After being at City for so long it was actually refreshing to be at a different club and see how things operate elsewhere. I was meeting different characters and learning about how they do things down there. Ian Holloway, Kenny Jackett and all the staff made me feel very welcome straight from day one.

It turned out to be two fantastic seasons at QPR and we gained promotion at Sheffield Wednesday on the last day of the 2003/04 season in very similar circumstances to the City and Blackburn game.

There was a great team spirit at QPR and no shortage of quality either. Paul Furlong was strong as an ox and absolutely fantastic for us up front, a 20-goals-a-season man. Kevin Gallen was Mr QPR, and there were players like Steve Palmer and Gareth Ainsworth, who has now moved into management. He is a good friend of mine who I'd played against previously when I was at City and he was at Port Vale.

We had a good laugh about it. We kicked lumps out of each other all game and both came off the field laughing because both our shirts were ripped to shreds. I tended to stick around with Gareth, mainly because he was a northerner among all these southern jessies and I could understand his accent!

Big Danny Shittu, a giant of a man. Marc Bircham, Dean Sturridge, Clarke Carlisle, who went on to become chairman of the PFA. Clarke had also suffered with a cruciate ligament injury just like myself and had been written off just like myself.

Clarke was living with Ralf Little from *The Royle Family* and *Two Pints of Lager and a Packet of Crisps* fame. Like me, he was a very northern lad living in the south.

I had Eve, I had stability in my private life and having been out of the game for so long, I really grasped this opportunity to play again with both hands and I wasn't going to let it get away from me. Clarke however was at a different place in his life. He was going through a bad time, hitting the bars three or four times a week and coming into training completely the worse for wear.

I would honestly say that drinking is, well was, at that time, absolutely prevalent among footballers, especially those who were lucky enough to have a few quid.

My room-mate was Paul Furlong, who was Chelsea's record signing at one stage and who I'd known before when I was on loan at Birmingham City. He was 36 at the time and scoring goals for fun. He was also a fitness freak and was really an example to young players of today of how you should look after yourself.

Paul would be in the gym after training, there would not be an ounce of fat on him and he was in the ice baths after a game, always doing things in the right way. He was the total opposite to Clarke, Mr Teetotal if you like, and compared to rooming with Kevin Horlock at least you'd be guaranteed a decent night's sleep!

We had Steve Palmer who had been a good player for Ipswich in the top flight, Tony Thorpe, a good attacker who I got on well with, and Jamie Cureton who had played Premier League football with Norwich at a time when the Canaries were going to places like Bayern Munich and winning away. It was a funny thing to see so many players with top-flight experience there.

The foreign imports were coming into the Premier League at the expense of our own players and the collapse of the ITV Sport channel had meant some players going abroad for a while to get games before they came back. So you could go right down the leagues and be surprised about some of the names you'd see on the teamsheets.

Also on the books at Loftus Road was Arthur Gnohere, who had spat at me while he was playing for Burnley previously. When I signed for QPR he was there and he came straight over to me and apologised for what had happened.

When I signed the season was already a couple of weeks old and the boys had already made a solid start. At the end of my first week I came on as sub in a 3-0 win over Chesterfield at Loftus Road. It certainly was great to be back.

For the first six months I was living in Ealing Common, near to the ground. Eve would come down and stay with me every other weekend at first until we found a place in Apsley Lock, near Hemel Hempstead, and she came to live with me there.

After training I would go home and have a run up and down the canals where I lived, using a heart rate monitor to test my fitness levels. That's if I wasn't still at the training ground doing a bit of extra work anyway.

At QPR we had a fitness coach called Scott Rushton, a former Army guy who was as strict as anyone I'd ever worked with.

We would do extra training in the afternoon. Extra weights in the gym to keep your strength up, more dips, more circuits. I didn't mind because I didn't know many people down there so I would have only been going home to an empty house or going in London spending money on things I didn't even need.

We did a lot of sports science work. We also had the introduction of ice baths straight after games to help our muscles heal.

Ian Holloway was a big fan of head tennis at the end of training. It hones your touch and balance and we would play two-touch over the net. It's a great fitness tool because you are always on the move. Ollie, Tim Breacker, Kevin Gallen and Marc Bircham were the best ones at head tennis.

At City it was daft with 50-odd players. At QPR you were always going to get a closer bond because with only 20 or so players you would get to know each other better and everyone became closer quicker.

With Ollie we'd do pyramid runs with parachutes on our backs. I always thought his training sessions were well thought-out. We were running 20 yards forwards then 20 yards backwards; 40 yards forwards then 40 yards backwards; then

60, 80 and finally 100 yards. We had to do all this within three minutes. They would run you really hard but you would have a laugh doing it rather than just running round and round and round a pitch like with other coaches.

On Thursdays and Fridays we might have a few words about the opposition and the people we should keep an eye on, or things the opposition players were doing. We would look at tactics and how we would approach a game, or video analysis of ourselves and of the players we would be coming up against next.

The only time in my career I had done anything which could be vaguely described as ball work, i.e. training with the ball, was under Juan Carlos Osario, the Colombian coach brought in under Kevin Keegan. It was weird at City. Keegan would do his thing then Osario would do his hour and you'd think, 'That's it, we're going home now.'

Then Stuart Pearce would come in and say, 'No, no, lads. We're not fit enough. We need to do some running, we've not done enough running today', and we'd do another half an hour.

You'd think it would be more organised at City but with so many coaches you didn't know what was what half the time. The ball work was good with Juan Carlos. I think a lot of us worked on our passing and close control with him. At QPR it was kept nice and simple which is all you want as a footballer – clear, easy instructions.

Ollie would continually keep us on our toes by trying new things out all the time. Very rarely would we have a day off. He was the same as Kevin Keegan in that regard but with Ollie, very occasionally he would just turn round and say, 'Come on lads, we're not training today', and just treat us all to a Nando's.

Ollie's focus would always be on the very next game. He has his way of doing things, wacky methods or whatever you want to call them, but on the whole they worked. On occasions he'd do stuff like take us to play golf. If we couldn't play on the training ground because of bad weather, we'd all do something indoors together. He made everyone feel involved. He was also on top of the Premier League at one time too, very briefly, with Blackpool on the first day of the season!

Shortly before this period in my life I was seriously contemplating leaving the game altogether even though I had just turned 29. I had felt as if I had been dumped on football's scrapheap and felt disillusioned by a game I once loved. I had even contemplated retraining and becoming a chef at one point.

Here I was falling back in love with football once again and it felt great. Ollie would make the lads laugh every day and I found his own particular brand of man-management to be excellent.

Training was really enjoyable too under Kenny Jackett. We would have regular meetings about games and watch videos and he was exceptionally thorough when it came to preparing the players. Kenny used to take the back four away for video analysis in our own group, looking back at how we worked together and what happened in the last game. It was a really professional set-up. They had the same training ground as the London Wasps rugby team and there was a chance to share facilities and expertise.

The Christmas do at QPR that year was down at the Hammersmith Palais on the Shepherd's Bush Road, a famous nearby venue, and they were having a school disco night. It's gone now but in its heyday it played host to The Beatles, The Who, The Sex Pistols and Joe Strummer sang about it in The Clash song 'White Man in Hammersmith Palais'.

It was well known in the area for being a lively event every Saturday so that's where we went. About 3,000 people were there, the majority of whom seemed to be women of the MILF/cougar vintage dressed up in school uniforms.

It was cheap and cheerful and with plenty to look at most of the lads were well pleased! Less so some of the players' wives and girlfriends who felt a bit unsure about themselves at such an occasion. Even though they were all dressed exactly the same.

My first knees-up at City was a Christmas bash where I was dressed as a daft schoolkid and here I was ten years later dressed in exactly the same clobber! Some things never change.

With the drink flowing and the music blaring you could kind of predict the dramas that were about to unfold. Some of the WAGs thought the players were a bit too keen on talking to some of the other clubbers – female ones – whenever any of them came over. So a group of wives headed off without the players and went into the West End, leaving the players to fend off the attentions of their newly-formed cougar fan club.

A couple of hours later some of the guys were getting calls and texts from other Premier League players – some of the most famous ones in the country – who had said some of the QPR wives were with them in a club and had been trying to get fresh with some of them so they were just letting us know!

Eve was well liked by all the other WAGs. She stayed out of the petty squabbles that you would occasionally hear about. She came across as self-assured and completely normal in the eyes of the other girls and they all flocked to her as they thought she was the coolest and most self-confident of them to be seen with.

QPR were a good club with a loyal local fanbase. Average crowds were around 17,000 and with Loftus Road being a tight little ground it was always a good atmosphere down there.

There was a bit of pressure around the place as they were in the third tier but there was a desire and a hunger among the players to bounce back after narrowly missing out in the play-off final the previous May. They had lost 1-0 to Cardiff in the Millennium Stadium in a game which must have felt like an away trip for them. They weren't taking on a team that day, they were taking on a whole city.

In Manchester you always had people wanting to talk to you about football. I'd go to Kendals and the guy outside selling flowers was a Blue and he'd always want to talk about the latest crisis engulfing the club.

I'd go in certain pubs or certain bars and felt that I was being dragged down by some people. In London you could walk down the street and not be recognised. It was a good time. I was out of that goldfish bowl known as Manchester football. It's a small city and everyone knows everyone else. A footballer breaks wind and the whole city knows about it within three minutes.

We drew City in the League Cup so it was a chance to give the fans a wave and come up against some of my former team-mates. Kevin Keegan was still in charge and it was an expensive line-up he named. We gave as good as we got but City just had too much firepower. They had a great forward line with Nicolas Anelka, Robbie Fowler and Trevor Sinclair all featuring. Shaun Wright-Phillips scored two goals and Jon Macken the other in a 3-0 win. I remember Joey Barton was giving me constant verbals throughout the game.

Ten years previously I had played for City against QPR in a crazy League Cup tie at Loftus Road which City won 4-3. Ian Holloway had been on the opposition side playing in midfield for QPR that night while Trevor Sinclair had played for Rangers.

QPR were not without their problems. I've mentioned Clarke Carlisle. Gambling was another vice rife in that dressing room. There was one player who loved a bet on snooker, horses…on anything. One Monday he told me the story of his weekend. Friday he lost £12,000. Saturday he won

£18,000. Sunday he bought a Range Rover. That very day he lost a further £12,000.

I found the R's to be a motivated bunch with some good senior pros and a lot of good young players. I couldn't understand why this club were so low down the league. Maybe the sale of Les Ferdinand to Newcastle was the beginning of the end of a cycle for them.

Looking around the dressing room though I was impressed with what I saw. Ollie was an infectious character who would bring the best out of the lads with focused training sessions and plenty of quiet words in your ear to build up your confidence.

Our game was mainly based around playing a pressing style of football but we had players who could mix it up. We used mainly a 4-4-2 formation with Paul Furlong, fit as a fiddle and a strong runner, leading the line. Good wingers in Kevin McLeod and Lee Cook provided the service.

Plymouth Argyle away was a top-of-the-table clash and we went down 2-0 at Home Park. They went on to win the league that year. Paul Sturrock, who went on to manage Southampton and return to Plymouth a few years later, was in charge and they had a good side. Plymouth had Nicky Weaver and Martin 'Buster' Phillips there and they both met me off the bus.

There were plenty of times that season when we got battered but we hung in there and fought, stayed in the game and came away with a result of some sort. It was a division where you had to earn the right to play.

The Sheffield Wednesday game is viewed by QPR fans as the start of a resurrection, the start of a comeback, a bit like how the 1999 play-off final is viewed by City fans.

We'd been bottling it for weeks. After Christmas our form was patchy at best. Three straight defeats on the road at Southend, Bournemouth and Chesterfield meant we were losing ground. We were conceding a lot of bad goals.

Three draws in the next five games was also a sign that we weren't getting things our own way and after a 2-0 win against Wrexham in mid-March we then hit the skids big time. Out of the next seven league games we won just once. We then lost that game at Plymouth.

In 1999/2000 we had a similar run like that in February and March of the promotion season with City when we returned to the Premier League. It was just a crisis of confidence at exactly the wrong time. At City the daft seven-game spell was five draws and two defeats; five points taken from 21 and 16 dropped. You would find though that you would drop points but everyone else would drop points. Things just happened like that.

There were two games left and we needed to win both. The first was at home against Swindon and we got a narrow 1-0 victory. Then we had to go to Hillsborough and get a result at Sheffield Wednesday. We were backed up there by 7,000 great fans. It was like the whole of west London had their day out up the M1.

Ollie got us all together as a team and gave a great speech. Are we good enough? Yes we are. Let's stick together and prove it. There were some older heads and some younger players who had never experienced a day like this before. The message was simple. Stay calm and trust each other out there.

On the day of the game I felt less pressure on me than some of the other players. I saw the similarities with the Blackburn match. I had been through a similar experience before and was remaining focused on that.

Ken Bates was in our hotel as I think he was involved in a bid to try and take over Sheffield Wednesday at the time. Then we went on to the ground and it was a bright, sunny day with everyone calm. The Rangers fans were there but it wasn't the chaos of Ewood Park.

It was a quiet dressing room beforehand. I was really calm but then I could feel a touch of nervousness – understandably – among some of the boys during the warm-up. I secretly felt we might bottle it.

As for the game itself, we played well in patches and scored the goals at the right times. Mr QPR himself, Kevin Gallen, scored first and a great turn and shot on the volley from our leading marksman Paul Furlong made it 2-0. Wednesday, featuring former City players Mark Robins and Terry Cooke in their side, pulled it back to 2-1 and it looked like it would be a nervous end to the game.

We weathered the storm and got a break with an own goal from Chris Carr that gave us the breathing space we needed. There were similarities with Christian Dailly and his own goal for Blackburn against City in 2000 as once that went in we kind of felt we were going to be OK.

It was a superb feeling at the final whistle and we went to celebrate with the fans. 'Holloway's blue and white army' was the chant as all the players piled on top of him.

I mentioned I was with Eve. Things had happened really quickly with Eve. I was in domestic bliss with her down in London and our love just blossomed. I'd split with a former girlfriend of nine years about three weeks previously. It had fizzled out and it hadn't really been going anywhere for quite a while.

I wasn't particularly looking for anyone at the time. Nor was I in the mindset of, 'I'm single, let's sleep with a hundred women before I pick somebody else.' I'm a laid-back kind of guy but I knew fairly quickly after meeting her that Eve was something special; that she was the one!

How did we meet? One of the shops I used to get my clobber from was a clothes shop up in Milnrow, a designer outlet in an old mill building. Eve used to work in the shop where I would go shopping. I'd only noticed her once before. I used to go in on a Sunday lunchtime, saw a nice girl smiling at me but didn't think anything of it. Eve was working there with her previous boyfriend for a while and coincidentally around the same time I finished with my previous partner, she too had just become single again.

I'd been in for some clothes one Sunday and the next day I was going out for training when Alex Stepney jogged up to me. 'Here, Edgy, you've got an admirer, you know that,' he said, and I just laughed. 'Who's that then Alex?' I asked and he said, 'The girl in the shop. That's Stuart's daughter.' Stuart's sister Sheila was married into Alex's family so Alex and Eve's dads knew each other. 'She really likes you. She wants you to give her a ring!'

By now I thought he was winding me up. 'Alex…I've only seen her behind the counter a couple of times.' 'But Edgy…she really likes you…and she's single.' The rest is history!

I just thought I would ring the shop and see what happens. I was sure though that it was some kind of practical joke but then I thought she was not bad looking so I would ring anyway.

It was very much like something at school. A two-minute conversation, like something at breaktime. Not a big conversation. 'All right, it's Edgy.' 'Oh hi!' 'Shall we go out then?' 'OK,' and then that was it. It wasn't a wind-up and I'd pulled a stunner!

We went to the pictures on our first date. I am 5ft 8in and she is taller than me anyway but turned up in a pair of cowboy boots with very high heels and must have been about 6ft 3in towering over me.

Things progressed quickly and after only a few months, with her parents away in America, I seized my opportunity. I had already decided that I was going to propose. I'd bought the ring but wasn't sure about asking her – let alone her dad first – so I just gave her a box and said, 'Here, Eve, have a look at that, that's for you', and she found the ring inside.

We got engaged while Eve's parents were away. When they came back off holiday they were obviously in for a nice surprise! We were all outside on the patio having drinks when they were back when I got up to go to the toilet. 'Oh Stuart, by the way, Eve's got something to tell you,' I said, and I hurried off to the toilet to let poor Eve gently break the news.

We'd been driving round everywhere trying to find somewhere to get married. We both had large families up north and as much as we wanted to invite everyone, unless we got married in a football stadium there would just be no way of accommodating everybody. So we ended up settling on this amazing place a few miles from where we live and we thought we needed sensible numbers but would let them all come down to us.

We eventually settled on The Grove, a luxury golf, spa and health resort in Hertfordshire. I'd been there before attending an England get-together. To be honest though, we didn't pick that place, it picked us. It was simply stunning.

Eve organised just about everything to do with the wedding. In true groom style I just sort of turned up on the day. Stuart had offered to pay for it but we said no, we would chip in too.

She chose the menus and the decorations, she went down for food tasting with her mum and dad. All the important little jobs. Eve sorted them all out. I circled our wedding date on the calendar so I would at least remember to attend!

There were around 100 guests including Kevin Horlock and Tony Grant from City and a few of the QPR lads including Tony

Thorpe who I hit it off with. I also invited the QPR physio who I'd not known long but who was amazing with me. I had real problems with my knee at times and he came up with a whole new exercise regime aimed on getting the knee back to where it should be.

I didn't really have a stag do as such. It was just a few drinks with a few select family members the night before in Watford. Then back to the hotel for a few.

Eve kept me waiting at the altar for ten minutes. Oh well, I suppose it's allowed!

Like anyone who has been through it, you have to prepare your speech and to be fair to my best man Steve he gave a fantastic speech of his own. It was very emotional. Both myself and Eve have some dear friends that go back to our school days and Steve is one of them.

For the honeymoon we went to Mauritius and it is definitely one of the best places we have visited. We enjoyed a really relaxing holiday. I didn't feel like a footballer, I just felt like a normal person, completely contented, able to enjoy a stress-free holiday and the start of married life.

There was plenty to do during the day. Eve is a sunbathing queen and just loves to chill out and sunbathe but I was out kayaking and doing other watersports. I would play golf and Eve would drive the buggy all the way round so it meant we could spend time together – however in the evening it seemed to be the same seven or eight couples that you would bump into.

The main room was a bar with low lighting and every night they had the same singer on, a guy who looked just like Errol Brown from Hot Chocolate who would be crooning away in the corner. There was nothing else to do then apart from sink cocktail after cocktail, vodka, gin and so on. There are only so many times you can stand hearing 'I believe in miracles' or whatever he was banging on about.

We also enjoyed a fantastic fly-drive holiday in America where we went coast-to-coast on Route 66. Happy days, and you have so much more time on your hands when you don't have kids!

Eve has two sisters, Rachel and Sophie, and Eve's mum Karen also hails from Milnrow. They were all big United fans before they met me… unfortunately some of them still are! We do see our parents quite a lot but the parents themselves don't often meet.

Many lads come into football and don't always have a secure family background. I have always been blessed in that regard though.

I remember the reaction when Eve became pregnant. We had been trying for a while. I remember even more vividly when she went into labour. Panic stations! By then I had learnt the art of pulling my weight around the house. I had left Bradford and had recently joined Macclesfield so I was already really thinking about my life after playing and that really meant being a father and a family man.

It all came at the right time for me. Players who were on even less than I was back in the old days really struggled when they finished playing as they didn't have a nest egg saved up or, if they didn't have family, they may have squandered it on drink. Many players got divorced soon after they finished as they would be so used to spending so much of their time without their wives. As soon as they hung their boots up and realised they had to spend time in the house they would be off out down the golf club or off having their flings.

I was fortunate that I was in the right place at the right time of my life to start my family with my wonderful life partner Eve and with everything that needed doing I was able to bring up my kids, Cassie and Olivia.

When Cassie was born I was still playing at Macclesfield but I have been able to see her and Olivia grow up. So many players miss out on so much of their children's development because of the overnight trips and the club commitments you have to perform. I miss playing, of course I do, but I have been able to experience and enjoy seeing the girls grow up and develop and what fantastic girls they are too.

I would have been quite happy in a way to stay at QPR beyond those two years if it wasn't for the pull of back home. Halfway through the second year I picked up a bad knock just before Christmas which meant I was out of action over the festive period.

I was meant to be playing over Christmas and the New Year so out of the blue all our plans were now changing. Eve was a bit homesick, missing her folks back home – as I was too – and suddenly we realised we didn't have to stay in London on our own, we could go back home and surprise everyone, so that's exactly what we did.

On Christmas Eve we drove home straight to Eve's parents and gave them a shock when they opened the front door. We stayed for Christmas Day and we had a great laugh and a wonderful time all round.

Although it was funny circumstances which had brought us back to the north-west it felt right and with one eye on being parents at some point in the near future and us realising we would need the support of a family network to help us, the decision to go back home was kind of made for us around then.

The lease on the flat was up in the summer and we felt sure as we got nearer to the date we would be moving, especially when I had one or two slight niggles which meant I struggled to get a look-in towards the end of the second year.

Eve came from a United-supporting family. Her dad was a regular at Old Trafford and had been going for years. One day he decided he would take up my offer of a ticket for a match. It was actually that game against West Brom on Boxing Day when I was sent off for two bookable offences.

I'd got Stuart tickets near the front of the main stand right near the tunnel. He was wearing a white leather jacket that day and when I was sent off he was going absolutely ballistic in the stand at the referee. The Sky cameras were following me as I walked down the tunnel and there's Stuart going nuts on television and all his Red mates in the pub are watching him. So his phone starts going. 'What are you doing there? We know you're at City…closet Blue.' After the game he was moaning, 'I can't believe they all saw me!'

14
SLIDE AWAY

MY next move was to a sleeping giant of sorts, Bradford City. A big club in their own right, they had always been outside the top flight really until the fairytale adventure into the Premier League at the turn of the millennium. At least that's what I kept telling myself. I was sliding down the leagues now, a lower-league player, and I had to accept that's where I was at.

Bradford are a club with a loyal fanbase who had been scarred so badly by the tragedy that gets so often overlooked, the awful fire of May 1985 which claimed the lives of 56 people. On the same day that happened Manchester City were wrapping up promotion to the tune of a 5-1 win at home to Charlton Athletic in a frenzied party atmosphere at Maine Road. *Match of the Day* that night showed scenes of ecstatic Blues swarming all over the pitch. Over the Pennines at Valley Parade people were burning to death in an old wooden stand.

The club and indeed the whole city had bounced back from that disaster into the top flight and of course players had come in on big money. Stan Collymore was just one very talented man who ended up at Bradford at one time.

They were sat in the third tier when I signed and the expectation of the fans was of a promotion tilt. They saw the Championship, as it was now known, as being the natural domain for Bradford City but the club had some financial problems and still had some big wage-earners on the books.

The move came about after I had bumped into Dean Windass out in Huddersfield one day. He asked me if I had got a club, I said I hadn't, so he said, 'OK, I'll ring the gaffer. Leave it with me.'

The gaffer in question was Colin Todd, the former Derby County and England man. A very 'old-school' manager but a nice guy nonetheless.

At the time and unknown to Dean I had been approached by Blackpool. Apparently Simon Grayson had asked about me and they were looking to put something together but Bradford were first on the scene and they came in quickly with a decent offer. It was close to home and I needed to keep playing.

Julian Rhodes was the club chairman and he was in the process of helping them battle against their financial problems at that stage so negotiations went on for a while before we got an agreement.

I could see something else happening here also. It wasn't particularly the case that I had an issue with playing my football in lower leagues as I got older, by now I had come to terms with that and knew that my best days were 'behind me', it was more the fact that unfortunately I had no real feeling for Bradford City. It was just somewhere to work. It was just another club.

I had been proud to play for Manchester City. They were – they are – my club. Queens Park Rangers was also a great move for me in so many ways and the fact I had to up sticks and live in London made me immerse myself in the club and get involved so I ending up having a lot of feeling for them and I still look out for their results now.

While I respected Bradford and their fans, it was just a place of work. When I was at City I used to get frustrated with the attitude of other players in our dressing room; players who had just come for the money and whose hearts weren't in it. At Bradford I am not saying my heart wasn't in it. I always gave my best and certainly never went there for the money. I just didn't feel the same way about the club though as playing for City.

Half an hour after a game I would be in the car and heading back home whereas if it was City or QPR, I'd hang around the players' lounge, stay to meet and greet fans, keep up to date with all the gossip from various friends I had about the place.

During my time at Bradford, Deano was sold to Hull, his hometown club. We missed his goal threat in the second year I was there. He was a big loss. He was a good lad and scored bags of important goals for us. In 2008 Deano ended up scoring the winner for Hull in the play-off final at Wembley and became a club legend there.

Deano is one of football's most interesting characters. He was released by Brian Horton of all people at Hull in his early days and was also sent off three times in one game! He liked a pint and at times, by his own admission, he suffered from a terrible temper. His problems have been well documented, not least by himself in his own book. He was a goal every other game man for us when he played at Bradford, his second spell with the club.

Footballers do have problems. Deano has been brave enough to talk about his. The alcohol. The depression. The suicide attempts. It's hard to believe that you go to work with these people and they are the most fantastic guys but inside, hidden away from everyone else, they've all got their own problems.

It's absolutely tragic. I read his article in the papers a few years ago when he said going into rehab saved his life.

There were still some big-name players at Bradford but financially the club weren't doing that well and had to rely on a funny mix of former Premier League players and a few kids.

Steve Claridge was there for a time while I was there. Steve has had more clubs than Tiger Woods! Moving around makes you so well connected in football. He's had a good TV career and always seems to talk sense.

David Wetherall was a club hero, having scored the winner against Liverpool in 2000 which kept Bradford in the Premier League in the most surreal of circumstances. We had Aguero v QPR and Dicky's goal v Gillingham. That was their magic moment. Fair play to them.

Dave was an experienced guy and a big character around the club. He wouldn't be shy of voicing an opinion. I, too, would voice an opinion but usually when I was asked for one while others, like Deano and Dave, would normally let everyone know theirs first.

Danny Cadamarteri, formerly of Everton, was there. Me and Danny shared something in common in that we both had Italian links on our mothers' side and Caribbean links on our fathers'. Here is another player who had his problems.

Danny was originally remembered as being a hero in the Merseyside derby for Everton but later on he failed a drugs test at Bradford after a game against Oldham Athletic. When you hear 'drugs' you think of cocaine or other such substances but in Danny's case it was decongestant he took for a cold which sealed his fate.

One familiar face for me was Bruce Dyer, who had been my room-mate during the England under-21 tournament in Toulon in 1994.

Bobby Petta, who had spells at Ipswich and Celtic, was also there. Bobby used to like a drink and he liked to chew tobacco. In fact he was always going round chewing tobacco, it must have been a kind of release for him. It was a bit strange but he was a nice guy.

I broke my leg playing for Bradford away at Colchester. It was a bad time for me injuries-wise anyway. I was always carrying a lot of niggly problems and never really getting over them so most of the time I was not 100 per cent fit when I played. I had hamstring strains and problems with my knee. I think I was never at the top of my game fitness-wise once I left QPR.

Colin Todd was very old-school when it came to training. It was 11 v 11, shooting, crossing and finishing, and no real variety. I found him a great guy to work with though.

I was pleased for Bradford when they reached the League Cup Final in 2013 against Swansea because it was a bit of glory and a few quid in the bank too.

One thing I noticed as I dropped down the leagues, and I found this to be the case at Macclesfield as well as Bradford, was the lower you went in football the more you had a lot of guys with big personal problems. They were spending more than they earned and had various insecurities.

Sometimes they were the young ones coming through and nobody at the club had given them advice on how to handle situations, what to do with money or what to do if something in their private life was affecting their mental state and performance on the pitch. Football is a very macho environment, especially in the lower leagues, and talking about personal problems, to some, may look like a sign of weakness.

Now and again I would join some of the more experienced players at Bradford and join them for a swift half after training and just chew over the fat. It could be about training or how the games were going but also it could be about issues one or two of the guys had and we tried to help out in a problem-aired-problem-shared kind of way.

I would meet up with guys like John Swift and Craig Bentham, young lads who were breaking through into the first team, and offer them some advice. A quick chat over a Guinness and a plate of sandwiches is all it takes to bond sometimes.

At Bradford and especially later when I went to Macclesfield I found that certain young players might be on more money than their mates outside of football but because they weren't on huge amounts more, they still had their friends which meant their builder mate who likes a line of coke at the weekend or their plumber mate who might be the one that can't walk away from a fight are still central in their lives. I came across lads who had problems at home.

Marc Bridge-Wilkinson wasn't always popular with some of the guys in the dressing room. He was just confident but some of the lads mistook his confidence for arrogance. I tended to bond with anyone who had played a higher level, like me. I didn't think I was superior to players who hadn't played the same level as me or who were just starting out in the game, it's probably just that I felt I had more in common with them – life experiences and experiences in football generally.

Deano was kind of a link between the managers and the players. He seemed to have a bit of clout there, he was on good terms with the chairman as well as the manager. Maybe the manager kept him onside so to speak as if results went against the manager perhaps Deano would have been a fans' favourite to take his job.

Being a parent focuses the mind on such a range of things. At Bradford I would go straight home after a game and carry on with my parenting duties. The one thing about my career starting to slide in my late 20s was that it was kind of a nice time to become a parent. If I was still at City I would have been earning more but would have had far less in the way of family time. There would have been more meetings, a more disciplined approach all round. More demands on your time.

15

THE MACC LADS ARE HAVING A PARTY

MY old mate Ian Brightwell offered me a lifeline when he took over the Silkmen of Macclesfield Town. The journey from the top to the bottom was nearing completion. From the Premier League to Macclesfield Town in just a few years.

I had my doubts but I went down to see Paul Lake, who was the physio there. Asa Hartford was also there as assistant to Brightwell, who we called 'Bob', so I felt a little happier seeing a couple of familiar faces there. It was an opportunity to carry on playing but it didn't quite feel right.

Bob and Asa wanted to play football on the deck but the players we had were conditioned to play a certain brand of football. I needed a club and at that time Macclesfield Town was a place to go for people from the Manchester football scene.

Ian Brightwell had taken over from Paul Ince. He in turn had taken over from Brian Horton and prior to Horton the man in charge was David Moss! Sammy McIlroy had put Macclesfield well and truly on the map and he was followed by Peter Davenport.

McIlroy did a magnificent job. The club had to win the Conference twice to actually get into the league as the first time they won it in 1995 the ground didn't meet the required standards. So they won it again two years later and by that time the ground was ready. On the crest of a wave the momentum continued and they then went straight up yet again and ended up in the same league as City for 1998/99.

The club were relegated in that season but with such small crowds at the Moss Rose you could say they absolutely over-achieved and they have never been able to get close to those glory days. It's a shame now that Macclesfield are outside of the Football League again.

They had stayed up by the skin of their teeth the season before I arrived there and that summer Bob took over in his first managerial role in football. He rang me up asking me how much I would need so I gave him a figure and he said, 'OK, leave it with me.'

I had literally been scratching around, doing my own training, keeping fit, playing golf, going swimming, going running. I'd asked Ian for about £900 a week but I think the budget for the squad for the whole year was only £650,000. So my wages were probably a sizeable chunk of their whole annual 'shoestring' budget.

Football was still recovering from the ITV Sport channel fallout but at least the club were being propped up by the Al Khadi money. The Macclesfield fans say at least Ian tried to get the team to play football. I keep alternating between Ian and Bob but it's the same person. The City fans know exactly what I'm on about!

As well as Bob, Asa and Paul at the club, we had Terry Dunfield the Canadian international, who I knew from City and only recently was playing at Oldham. We had a couple of lads up front in Franny Green and Gareth Evans. There was plenty of endeavour and effort from those two and no little skill. Overall perhaps our squad lacked a bit of pace.

Ian played at the back with a lad called Sean Massey who arrived at the club from Chester. Sean had apparently done a Luis Suarez while at Chester and bit a Stockport County player, earning himself a ban.

The club couldn't afford to risk a repeat of the struggles of the previous season. For whatever reason things weren't going our way though and the board decided to make the change.

When Ian left as manager I was left there on that wage and the next managerial team who came in, Keith Alexander and Gary Simpson, probably felt I was a burden for them and was taking up too much of their budget. Average wages I guess in that squad might have been around £300 a week. I didn't know that at the time when I negotiated with Ian.

It was funny because I had always been one of the lowest-paid players at City and by the time I go somewhere on the best money, it's at Macclesfield and I feel like a bit of a spare part around the place.

Playing in the lower leagues was the biggest eye-opener ever. I went down to the Moss Rose and had a look around. The dressing room was tiny. There was one exercise bike which was about 50 years old and didn't even work!

I didn't enjoy the type of football played at that level or indeed playing at that level. Crash bang wallop, this was League 2 football.

In the lower leagues it's weird. For me personally the injuries I had picked up really robbed me of the pace I once thrived on. So you kind of rely on speed of thought to get you through games. I was actually more composed on the ball, my distribution was excellent. I think my passing improved as I got older. I learnt how to adapt because you got less time on the ball in the lower leagues, you were pressed quicker so you had to ensure your distribution out from the back was efficient.

Keith Alexander took over and on his first day in charge in his very first meeting with the players he just said, 'Hello, my name is Keith Alexander and this is my assistant Gary Simpson and if anyone doesn't like it here they can fuck off!'

The ITV Digital crash hadn't left me with many options apart from playing in a team whose main tactics at the time were to just impose themselves physically on the opposition, cropping players, elbows flying, long-ball football. I felt surplus to requirements as soon as Brightwell had left. The fans were unhappy with the brand of football too.

The new manager didn't even give me the time of day. He knew I was someone who had played at a higher level. He never asked my opinion on anything football-related in all my time there. I felt I was being messed about at times. One day in the build-up to an important game he pulled me to one side and said he was going to change the system and wanted me to play at centre-half. We then worked on that in training. Come the matchday I wasn't even involved with the squad.

It was all about winning the second ball. Knock it long and win the second ball. Make the other team come out to play and then win it back off them. There were statistics around to say more goals were scored when you knocked it long.

Knowing you were not part of the manager's plans, even at that lower level, was especially demoralising. I had grown up loving the game of football but many times in my life football the game had hurt me and this was another such time.

I used to get on the bus and travel to away games. At times I was merely a travelling roadie and sometimes I wouldn't even need to get changed. I had been a kid on the bus with City's senior pros and had to brew up for them and show them some respect. I had kids on the bus with me at Macclesfield and they wouldn't bat an eyelid at me walking past them, such was the drop in my standing. If I had asked them to brew up for me – not that I did though – they would probably have just tutted and told me to do it myself.

I'd take my own kit home and wash it. I didn't mind that as much, it was just the general scenario of being stuck there that was getting me down. My career was going down the pan and the end of the road was looming.

Team talks were just about screaming at players. Very little in the way of tactics, it was just all about tempo, commitment, dominating the opposition and winning your individual 50-50 battles all over the pitch.

There was a particularly bad 5-0 defeat at Mansfield Town but we bounced back the following week with victory over Brentford, though that was the game in which I broke my ribs.

By now I was taking longer to get over injuries and became a little slower after each knock. I'd had a few and it was years since I had been at my peak physically.

It was an awful time for me personally. You are uncertain. It was a case of counting down towards the end of the season and you place your trust in agents to come up with options for you but it was beginning to dawn on me that this could be the end. As the weeks moved on I became resigned to the idea and then just became happy with that being the case.

In the last game of the 2007/08 season, against Chester, a 0-0 draw, I was booked in the last five minutes of the match. Although we were safe from relegation that booking, my fourth of the season, must have meant Macclesfield had reached a certain number of cautions and that would mean a fine for the club. Gary Simpson was cursing me after that and I just felt like I didn't need it anymore.

I didn't have a job to fall back on but I had some savings and a PFA pension. I was only 34 but in a way I was relieved to be retiring from football.

16

A SIGHT FOR SORE EYES

WHAT a lucky lad I am. Believe it or not I actually get paid to watch Manchester City. I do various roles behind the scenes at the club including matchday meet and greet and while it took some time the Blue Moon has finally well and truly risen.

The Arabs haven't got bored and the club haven't squandered the money. World-class players don't turn us down anymore, they want to play for us, and best of all, the supporters have their pride back after wondering for so long if the club would ever fulfil its potential.

You see City shirts everywhere now. You always saw a good amount anyway but you see a lot more now. Of course we've got new fans. Success brings that but we've had fans in this city who have had to play second fiddle to the other lot for far too long and these days it's just great to be a Blue in Manchester. This is our city.

What a difference there is now when you think of Manchester City, what a buzz Sheikh Mansour and his team have created about our club. We are a world name now. You can go anywhere in the world and they will have heard of Manchester City. United fans used to chant 'City, Manchester City…nobody knows their name' but that's all changed. Not only are we big news, we are exciting to watch.

I am not exactly sure if Sheikh Mansour did go to Spain in a Lamborghini and bring back a manager in Manuel Pellegrini but the club did decide to go all 'holistic' with a new approach even though it meant dispensing with the services of a title-winning boss, Roberto Mancini. The 'gamble' if you want to call it that has paid off. With his quiet and composed manner the City fans call Pellegrini 'This Charming Man' after The Smiths song.

'Bobby Manc', the guy who would never be seen without a City scarf around his neck, kept his promise and was the man who tore United's banner down and as a result will always have a special place in the hearts of City supporters.

The Pellegrini team is simply a joy to watch though. He inherited a lot of these players from Mancini but they just play with so much more freedom now. The movement is fantastic, so fluid.

We may not have a team full of homegrown Mancunians like we did in the era of Paul Lake, David White and Andy Hinchcliffe but with guys such as Vincent Kompany and Pablo Zabaleta around you have people who really love the club and who know what it's like to be a Blue.

You can see the brand of football we are trying to instil in players is welcomed more by them. Perhaps they just needed a more relaxed style around the club and around the training ground, and to be trusted more on the field. There's less tension about the place. The lads are playing for the manager.

Even at press conferences it's very rarely Pellegrini gets rattled. Unless it's after an appalling performance from a

Swedish referee. You can't read him. The press try to get him to bite but he just takes it all in his stride and he has earned the respect of the press now.

Look at what he did in the Champions League with clubs such as Malaga. Given time and resources let's see what he can do at City.

Certain players have improved under Pellegrini. Players such as David Silva and Aleksandar Kolarov found a second wind under him, as did Samir Nasri. Then you've got Fernandinho, a fantastic acquisition who covers every blade of grass. He offers tremendous work-rate which gives the likes of Yaya Toure a little bit more time on the ball.

Alvaro Negredo – what an impact he made in his very first season. No settling-in period required there was there. Stevan Jovetic too has shown glimpses of promise when he has had an opportunity.

I feel those players were always capable of playing this style of football but maybe it needed the change of manager to help deliver that. No more running up the hill at Carrington!

Not only is it a different style of football we are seeing, it's been a different style of man-management as well. We've had people like Brian Kidd who know the DNA of the club and even though he scored in the European Cup Final for Manchester United, he has always had a lot of affection for Manchester City in the same way Denis Law does.

Kidd and Law are really unique in that they are loved and admired by both sets of supporters in Manchester. Kiddo has got to be one of the best assistant managers in the game.

We are much more of a forward-thinking team, so solid on the break when other teams lose the ball. I would have loved to have played in a team like this, in an era such as this where the focus is about getting forward all of the time. Not as much bodily contact, fighting, tussling or hacking people down after ten yards. Just going out and being able to express yourself.

I have my coaching classes that I run and I go into various schools across Greater Manchester. I see a big difference in terms of behaviour patterns now between the kids in the various areas that I coach in.

I go into schools in Harpurhey, north Manchester, with two learning mentors, Adam and Shaun, and also in the Rochdale area. Doing football training is the reward after classroom-based studies have finished. I cover some lunchtimes and some after-school classes and they are all ages from five through to 11.

Often kids have their own issues from home; their parents have split up, or they have attendance or motivational difficulties. Football is a good outlet to do some good and helps people integrate.

One thing that seems to be apparent is that City are winning back the kids in Manchester. There was a generation where we had to fight for every supporter as we underachieved as a club. Not any more. They all love City and want to play for the club. They all want to go on the tour and be shown round the Etihad.

I also coach college teams from Saudi Arabia who would all be academy standard over here.

One thing which is very unique about Manchester City, even in this day and age where the club has changed beyond all reasonable recognition, is that they have a very strong and mainly locally-based supporters' organisation which gets visits from the former players. That is nice because it maintains that bond between the players and the supporters. You can't really expect today's first-team players to feature much at meetings given the demands on their time. Media commitments are especially busy but they play all days of the week now and plenty of rest after training is paramount if performance on the pitch isn't to suffer.

A lot of the former players have done a great job over the years going around the branches. Alex Williams MBE, Paul Lake, Paul Power, Gary Owen, Peter Barnes, Ian Brightwell, David White, Andy Morrison, Shaun Goater…the list is endless but they go to see the supporters because they want to give something back to the fans who backed them.

A good mate of mine has just left the club and he went out at the top. That was Les Chapman, or 'Chappy' as he is known the world over. He came in as reserve team manager under Peter Reid and served under Brian Horton before he was sacked by Alan Ball. He then came back as kitman about a year later and has stayed ever since.

We used to share lifts into training together. We'd often stop at the bookies on the way to training so he could put his bets on, or simply stop at the paper shop so he could get a *Racing Post*.

One day he reversed into the bay window of my house and smashed his own rear windscreen. 'Don't worry Edgy, it'll be all right, I'll sort it,' he said and just drove off laughing!

Chappy is one of the unsung heroes in football. Every club needs them. He's a football person. He's a realist. He's played the game, managed and done all sorts of different jobs. He knows how footballers tick and how they think about things. You ask the players if they'll miss Chappy. He looked after their every need.

I was one of those players who would always be intrigued to see what sort of kit we had before the new season started. Each time a new kit was revealed I couldn't wait to see what it was like.

Funnily enough the one kit I never really took to was the Kappa kit, the one that everybody else seemed to rave about. The shorts were a bit tight for me and that's nothing to do with the size of my backside!

When I first broke through into the first team, Umbro manufactured the kit and you would get asked what size you needed, but for some reason we'd end up with kits that were all near enough the same size and the likes of me and Terry Phelan would have to fold the bottom of our shirts up two or three times at the bottom so they would fit into our shorts. Nowadays the kits are skin-tight and designed to let more air in, so the players are comfortable. Twenty years ago the kits were anything but comfy.

I have played against so many good players and tested myself against them. David Ginola, Robbie Keane, Craig Bellamy, Ryan Giggs, Lee Sharpe, Steve McManaman and Robbie Fowler all come to mind. Fowler scored six against us in a 6-0 win at Platt Lane in a B team match. We were both about 17. I was playing centre-half that day although not marking Fowler directly I should add!

Andy Sinton, Ian Wright, Paul Merson, Andy Cole, Jurgen Klinsmann, and David Speedie were all difficult opponents. Ian Rush and John Barnes at Liverpool. Paul Gascoigne at Everton. Even Tony Cottee and Graeme Sharp, they were a handful. I played against those two at the same time when they were coming back from injury in a reserve game.

Even though I have been booed by a section of fans I have always been happy to spend time in the company of City supporters and try to show them the type of guy I am. I've been round most of the supporters' club branches but you are sober and they've tended to have a few pints so you get asked really direct questions at times. You've got to expect that and respect that they have the right to ask anything they want, as long as it's not malicious.

It's the same now when I work in the executive lounges at the Etihad. I could be rubbing shoulders with Tony Book, Colin

Bell, Mike Summerbee or Tommy Booth. Lakey said to me on the first day of this role that 99 per cent of the supporters are great with you, asking for pictures or an autograph. In the main they are knowledgeable fans so they tend to be able to hold a decent conversation with you.

A lot of them want to talk to you about the Gillingham game. Some ask about other career highlights. If they are City fans they tend to know their stuff. Sometimes guests will be on the tables who aren't actually City fans. Paul Lake has had it, and it's soul-destroying where one throwaway remark can cut you apart. 'Who are you then?' 'How many games did you play for the club then?' 'Were you any good?'

You get the odd one who takes it too far, or others who are prim and proper and not even interested in the game at all. They are more interested in having a nice meal in the wonderful facilities we enjoy on the corporate side now at the club.

Matchday hospitality and the revenue it brings is so important to the club. When I first started training with City and Peter Swales was the chairman, there were no corporate facilities at all at Maine Road. They had to put people on a bus to a city centre hotel, wine and dine them then put them all back on the bus back across town and into the ground where we would no doubt get beat!

Just to reiterate the point about how great City fans are, I will mention the bond they often develop with certain players. They never forget the contribution you make. In the run to the 2011 FA Cup Final, Pablo Zabaleta's father was very ill back home in Argentina and he had some time at home but then had to fly back for the semi-final against United. He put a note on his Twitter account about his father and immediately thousands of City fans sent him goodwill messages, urging him to win the cup for his dad and fly back home to Argentina and show him that medal.

That cup run saw the passing of one of the club's most well-loved sons, Neil Young. He was the top scorer four years running during the Mercer–Allison years and a scorer of important goals including the winner in the 1969 FA Cup Final, up at Newcastle in the title decider in 1968 and, of course, in the European Cup Winners' Cup Final in Vienna against Gornik in 1970.

Neil's FA Cup winner was against Leicester and when City were paired against the Midlands side in January 2011 the supporters immediately thought of Neil, who at the time was gravely ill and days away from death. In terms of timing it seemed like fate but never ones to miss an opportunity, the City fans dressed themselves in the red and black colours that Neil had so gracefully won in 1969 and sang his name, not just in the Leicester tie but also at Wembley too in the final.

The winner at Wembley, which ended that 35-year trophy drought, was an identical strike to Neil's, a thundering left-footed drive from the edge of the box, albeit at the other end of the ground. It was scored 42 years after his goal and was scored by the number 42 on that day, Yaya Toure. Makes you think doesn't it.

Ask Uwe Rosler what he thinks about City fans. When he became ill with cancer and was going through chemotherapy the supporters rallied round him and sang his name at home matches. Then there was Mike Doyle. A Mancunian, a true Blue and a man who won everything at the club, and again the City fans showed their appreciation by honouring him at the 2014 League Cup Final against Sunderland as Doyley was the captain fantastic who led them to victory in the 1976 final and also scored in the 1970 win over West Brom.

So you see, far from being gloryhunters, the vast majority of Manchester City fans are and always have been really great supporters.

And what a career I had. I played during a time when the club was falling apart and divided but then pulled together like never before. I played under three different chairmen, under nine different managers if you include caretakers and in three different divisions. I scored two goals. One was at Wembley under extreme pressure and one was in our promotion campaign against Blackburn, a season where I would later captain the club back to their rightful place in the Premier League.

I've had the odd argument on Twitter. It was bad enough getting abuse when I was playing. People used to wait for me to make a mistake then get stuck in to me. I stopped playing years ago and occasionally I still get stick! 'You are one of the ones who took us down to the Second Division!' 'Edghill you were rubbish!' I just block them now. Luckily there are enough decent City fans around to educate these internet warriors.

Yes we have more success now and yes, the money is totally different. I'd play these days for the money…but would I get a chance as a youth team player to play in the first team anyway?

I loved Maine Road and having that as my place of work. I always showed an interest in what the office staff would be doing to support the on-field activities. I would treat everyone as an equal, take the mickey and have the mickey taken out of me in equal measure and I would always stand up and be counted when it came to attending a sponsorship event or a lottery function.

Players do get treated better these days. They get told they don't have to do interviews. Player liaison officers do everything for them. I am comfortable going on the radio or speaking on the television but I never had media training. We just used to go shopping in town after training.

Another difference from my days in the top flight is the referees. Nowadays they are celebrities. Back then, hardly anyone knew who they were.

I think the refs were better a few years ago. Dermot Gallagher, he was good. Tough but fair. You had the odd one like Jeff Winter who just seemed to want to hog all the limelight for himself and perhaps someone like Phil Dowd is the nearest you'd get to him now.

You want a referee who can talk to the players, who won't talk down to you as if they are a schoolteacher and you are in detention. You can't even tackle these days. Some of the referees who book players willy nilly now would not have lasted five minutes in the old days because they would have sent everyone off. Do they get told how to speak to players and listen to the points players make?

Nowadays they will train with clubs and get lots of information on players. They give talks to players at the start of the season on what's acceptable and what's not but then come the season it all seems to go out of the window.

Anyone who knows me, really knows me, will know what sort of guy I am. Yes, 'Edgy' could be an appropriate name in some ways because it is fair to say that sometimes people meeting me for the first time might find an 'edge' to my personality but appearances can be deceptive and underneath all that people will find a caring and warm character with a dry sense of humour. A trouble-causer? No, not in a million years.

I get more satisfaction now from people asking for a photo on their phones or an autograph. I appreciate it more because I have stopped playing and am out of that protected bubble of football and mixing with everyday people again. It's not an ego thing per se but people saying 'hello' in the supermarket or on holiday, I don't mind that because it means they remember me.

I played for a long time and went to lots of fans' meetings. I played at a special time. However it's only when you retire and look back on your career you kind of realise what an important role you play in other people's lives. As players we live in a closeted bubble.

The letters I received, I really appreciated them at the time. I appreciate them even more now that I have retired. Letters from people of all ages. I dig them out occasionally and read them. To those fans, I was somebody. People used to pay their money to see you perform. For us it was a career and for them it was their life.

Yes I have felt the wrath of supporters but I have also felt their warmth and been carried off the field during pitch invasions by fans who appreciated my efforts. I have heard them sing my name. I stayed loyal to the club when I could have moved on and the club stayed loyal to me during difficult times such as my injury.

I have played alongside some fantastic and some not-so-fantastic players and have seen the ups and downs of football. The highs were gloriously high and the lows were oh so low.

When you look back at some of those dark times and compare them to now you realise someone very young supporting City will only have known good times. The City fans, even in those days, never hired a plane to try and get rid of the manager though.

I have always been involved with charities throughout my career and both myself and Eve have done events for the benefit of the NSPCC.

I look out for the results of all the clubs I played for, notably Queens Park Rangers, but the club in my heart is Manchester City. Once a Blue, always a Blue as they say.

Thanks for reading my story.